HATCHING BUTTERFLIES

Transitioning from a Corporate Career to a Self-Determined Future

SANDHYA VASUDEVAN

STARDOM BOOKS

www.StardomBooks.com

STARDOM BOOKS
112 Bordeaux Ct.
Coppell, TX 75019, USA

Copyright © 2024 by Sandhya Vasudevan

All rights reserved. No part of this book may be reproduced or used in any manner without written permission of the copyright owner except for the use of quotations in a book review.

FIRST EDITION MARCH 2024

STARDOM BOOKS, LLC.
112 Bordeaux Ct. Coppell, TX 75019, USA

www.stardombooks.com

Stardom Books, United States
Stardom Alliance, India

The author and publishers have made all reasonable efforts to contact copyright holders for permission and apologize for any omissions or errors in the form of credits given. Corrections may be made to future editions.

HATCHING BUTTERFLIES
Transitioning from a Corporate Career
to a Self-Determined Future

Sandhya Vasudevan

p. 205
cm. 13.97 X 21.59

Category:
BUS012000 Business & Economics: Careers – General
SEL027000 Self-Help: Personal Growth – Success

ISBN: 978-1-957456-41-6

DEDICATION

To all those who shaped me, with Eternal Gratitude.

The soul is an adventurer in life
Coming from the Ether to
Manifest Soul's desire / aspiration

A life well lived in time and space.
When the journey ends the
Form reverts back to Fire and
Merges with Water and Air
The meagre bones become the planet's substance again.

The Joy, the Love, the Caring lives on
Like a warm and protective embrace
Across Time and Space once more.

ENDORSEMENTS

"I had the pleasure of working closely with Sandhya for several years and was always struck by, and benefitted from, her meticulous eye for detail, principled approach & sense of balance. And yet as I started to read 'Hatching Butterflies', I honestly wasn't sure what to expect!
As I progressed through the book, my sense of wonder did not diminish. Each one of us, at different stages of our life, have to transition professionally, emotionally, culturally etc. and Hatching Butterflies provides a remarkably mature & insightful roadmap and the tools on how to transit successfully and with the least possible friction.
Starting with the powerful concept of PGROW, the book is an enlightened & practical guide on how to not only deal with change, but also profit from it. It strips out all vestiges of negative emotion from situations of adversity and disruption and, in fact, highlights the necessity to "self-disrupt". The consequence management of that is brilliantly addressed through vital initiatives like developing competencies, building networks (including a "challenge network" that keeps you on your toes and inculcates a growth mindset). While Sandhya dwells at length on the importance of "goal orientation", her sense of balance manifests itself as she nudges the reader with the "you are more than your career" chant.
Equal importance is attached to physical well-being, spiritual health and social capital. The ability to drill down to granular detail and then couple it with lateral thinking is one of the outstanding features of this brilliant book. Sandhya was, at one time, the only lady on the bank's Executive Committee. And while she was never quite a feminist, she was always

very sensitive towards gender related issues. This surfaces periodically in her book and rightfully so given that our perspectives, challenges and responses are seldom gender-neutral. Although the wisdom in this book is timeless, the period that it spans ran parallel to the pandemic. Those were difficult & uncertain times and during the course of which Sandhya also lost her enduring hero, her father. While the sense of loss is palpable, she doesn't depart from the path of objectivity and remains admirably constructive. She steadfastly advocates resilience, a growth mindset and a sense of purpose to emerge from the turbulence of change and successfully adapt to your new reality or, as they say, the new normal. At first glance Hatching Butterflies may come across as a survivor's guide for dealing with professional disruption, forced or voluntary. However, it is in fact a treatise on managing broader transformation and touches every aspect of life and our different touch points with the world. Sandhya had a stellar career and ran several senior management roles in which she was regularly confronted with challenging situations and complex people's issues. She, therefore, has a deep & rich reservoir of experience and insight to draw upon and share. However, in the book she goes well beyond that & reinforces her own learnings with domain expertise from subject matter experts as also her incisive observations from the extensive network she has so thoughtfully created. The end result is a book that will create a more holistic & contemporary genre in change management.

A very important element of being a good leader is 'self-leadership'. Hatching Butterflies is the most definitive work that I have read on that subject in a very long time. "

Ravneet Gill
Sports & Esport Education and Competitive Esports Entrepreneur
Former CEO Deutsche Bank India & Yes Bank
http://linkedin.com/in/ravneet-gill-532704122

"This is a fantastic informational book on how to create a career that matches your life's purpose. One of the best things is that it's also an activity book, and you can plan, act and transform as you read along. Sandhya's light and honest style of writing makes difficult concepts understandable and actionable. I would recommend it to anyone who feels they have a purpose to create a positive change in the world."

Kinga Papp, B.A., N.D., Dip.Kin.
ICPKP Faculty
Therapist. Coach. Teacher.
www.kingapapp.com

"In 'Hatching Butterflies,' Sandhya masterfully guides readers through the exhilarating journey of transitioning from a structured corporate career to a self-determined future. Her insightful narratives, filled with personal anecdotes and practical strategies, make this book a must-read for those yearning to embrace entrepreneurial freedom. Sandhya's deep understanding of the challenges and rewards of this metamorphosis offers both inspiration and tangible advice. Anyone contemplating a leap into the entrepreneurial world should read this book, not only to motivate but also equip you with the tools to gracefully navigate and succeed in your new, self-crafted path."

Ashutosh Garg
Founder, "The Brand Called You; Founder, Guardian Pharmacy"
www.linkedin.com/in/coach-ashutoshgarg/
ashutoshgargin.wordpress.com
ashutoshgarg56.blogspot.com
www.eQuationCoaching.com
www.tbcy.in
https://www.amazon.com/author/ashutoshgarg

"Sandhya has weaved a beautiful tapestry of her experiences and her journey. The book showcases Sandhya's experiences, her journey, her trials and triumphs. I highly recommend this book for people who are undergoing transitions in life, whether those changes are personal or professional. This book will be your personal change management journal."

Dhruti Shah
Director at C2C-OD | Author of The Resilient Entrepreneur| Leadership Coach
www.linkedin.com/in/dhrutis

CONTENTS

	Acknowledgments	i
	Foreword	iii
	Introduction	1
1	The Transition: Goals and Current Reality	5
2	You are more than your Career	31
3	Values And Beliefs: The "Why" Of Goals	57
4	Choice to Decision-Making	79
5	Networks: The Hidden Influence	99
6	Thriving In Uncertainty	123
7	Purpose: Your Bedrock To "Change"	143
8	Being a Woman Professional	163
9	Call To Action: Way Forward	175
	Appendix	185
	About the Author	189

ACKNOWLEDGMENTS

To the Stardom Team, Raam Anand who reached out to me asking me to write and the dedicated team of Ranjitha Vijaykumar, Rekha Krishnaprasad, Aditi Ajith Kumar, and H K Tejas.

My parents, aunts and cousins who are my bulwark without whom I cannot function and who have been my tribe since childhood.

My YPO forum buddies and friends for their irreverent and wise insights.

All my fellow travelers in life who have shaped me through various life lessons in the different companies that I have worked for and the industry forums I have engaged with.

Special thanks go to Professor [Dr] Vasanthi Srinivasan from IIMB for her forward and her incisive feedback; Ravneet Gill for his endorsement who gave me the confidence that the book could be immensely useful. Dhruti Shah took the pen to paper for me to fine-tune the book! Kinga Papp for her support; Ashutosh Garg who was the first to come back with his endorsement; Sophie Hutcheson for the feedback and endorsements and Rahul Pandey for the last-minute support.

To America's Got Talent – where I heard the phrase "Hatching Butterflies" and it seemed totally apt for the book, as I was visualizing 'from egg to pupae to butterfly' for the cover. It was serendipitous.

FOREWORD

The title of the book "Hatching Butterflies" is an interesting metaphor; the term "hatching" refers to the process of a caterpillar breaking out of an egg. Butterflies emerge through metamorphosis; they transform. Using the term hatching with butterflies suggests an interesting action. Several years ago, a student asked me if there was a difference between change and transition. At that time, I said change is external, and transition is internal.

Over the years, particularly during Covid, the distinction emerged. When the context changed, we adapted our ways of living and being, yet very few of us could make the internal identity transition as quickly. The external environment induces change and adaptation; it is a reaction. Transition is an inner journey requiring self-awareness, reflection, introspection, and willingness to shift thinking and acting. This book focuses on identity shift and provides a vocabulary to articulate the transition for anyone who intends to do so.

I have known Sandhya since 2008 and have seen her effectively navigate her professional challenges. Events like a company merger and subsequent role redundancy, feeling a sense of ennui in the work organization, and looking for a new role are all a part of the professional journey for leaders. These changes require new mindsets, ways of thinking, skills and competencies, and networks. Training programs, developmental interventions, mentors, and allies are required support that can help you succeed. However, managing an illness and navigating a senior executive role or relocating to a new city with significant elder care responsibilities are fundamental and dramatic changes, often unanticipated in the linear progression of life. Such significant events force you to confront your widely held beliefs and assumptions and, in the process, force you to reinvent yourself.

Identity transitions require you to spend long periods altering old values and engaging with new ones. Existential questions such as "Who am I?" and "What is the purpose of life?" have no easy answers and are ongoing and relentless throughout the journey. This exploration phase requires resilience and personal agency. Through the anecdotes, Sandhya gives a quick glimpse into her professional and personal transition journey.

The book also provides tools, techniques, and resources that help navigate the transition. Professionals can use these resources to enable their professional and personal journeys. The PGROW model that has helped Sandhya in her journey offers a very simple and pragmatic approach to evaluating personal and professional decisions.

The takeaway for any reader is that they can resonate with the journey and choices of being a leader and that reframing life events is crucial to managing personal and professional transitions.

Vasanthi Srinivasan
Professor – Organizational Behavior and HRM
Indian Institute of Management Bangalore

INTRODUCTION

In May 2017, my Dad fell ill. He was 89. As we got ready to go to the hospital, he thought we were going to the temple and could not comprehend why we just drove past it.

With a lump in my throat, I felt my whole world shake. It was as though a huge tree was beginning to be uprooted, and I was trying my small bit to hold it up.

Just like a frog that does not recognize slowly boiling water, my parents were aging, and I did not want to accept it.

Although no child aspires to be the 'parent' yet, that role falls on us. My Dad was never going to be as independent as he had been. My mother was emotionally vulnerable, and I could not be sure of her ability to handle the matters as before.

The daily influx of minor crises needed my constant attention, and I needed a more involved and proactive approach.

Despite past ups and downs, I knew they would not bounce back this time, and I would need to be their ballast going forward. While grateful for their support for so many years, it was still painful to recognize the shift in our journey, which started as parents caring for me to being adults engaging equally, and now I was the caregiver.

The acceptance of the new reality goes through its usual phases of denial, a sense of loss/ anger, to final acceptance of the New Reality.

At this point in my career, I was an MD who was the Deutsche Bank India's Regional Management COO and CRO with a commuting lifestyle – I would fly every Monday morning to Mumbai and return on Friday nights to Bangalore. This was no longer going to be possible, and I had to look for other options to manage my career. Many suggestions were made:

- Move your parents to Mumbai – *didn't want to uproot them.*

- Quit your career for now; it will be easier – *I didn't think I would be able to get back if I dropped out professionally at this point.*

- Find an alternate role in Bangalore that did not entail that much travel – *easier said than done!*

The harsh truth was, when I looked around for a role, there did not seem to be anything out there, and even when talking to people, it was not going anywhere. As a good friend said, for which I will always be grateful: "Sandhya, you are leading with your need to relocate to take care of your parents and not what you can contribute to the organization. Everyone wants someone who puts the organization first".

Often, the stressful situation blinds us to what the world needs from us vs. what has changed in our lives – be it a new baby, loss of a loved one, illness, or any other situation.

I was fortunate to find a global/regional role within Deutsche Bank as the Divisional Control and Regulatory Officer.

Yet more adjustments were needed: I focused on only 3 areas- Work, Home, and Self.

- Work: Thanks to 30 odd years, the ability to focus and leverage my competence enabled me to operate in the new role with reasonable ease.

- Home: this was a tough adjustment mentally, emotionally and physically.

- Self-care was vital. This meant that I prioritized health [exercise – yoga/Taiichi/qigong; food/supplements, etc.] and dropped all energy-draining activities; reading/ podcasts and videocasts were essential to nourish my mind, as were music and art. All were in place to keep me in balance. Yet, the most essential was the support system of family/friends.

These kinds of difficult situations occur in everyone's lives and often multiple times. Each time, we need to re-set to handle this new marathon – no, it's not a sprint!

These life events will impact our professional journey, and we need to build resilience to handle it.

Covid came, and with it, all our collective fears and stress increased. My Dad passed away quietly at home during the lockdown in September 2020. I am eternally grateful that he did not need to go through the horrors of hospitalization during Covid.

Despite the lockdown, I had enough support to deal with the grieving process, and I thought I would just carry on with my work.

Yet, a few months later, I felt it was time to shift out of the rhythm I had fallen into.

I have often noticed that when it is time to change, many things seem out of sync, and at work, we will often attribute it to work not being interesting, lack of support for growth, or the boss/ co-workers being unsupportive.

Even if any or all of them are true – if we are centered and in harmony with ourselves, we can handle everything.

This book is my exploration of the next couple of years of how I moved forward and some of the tools and approaches that I have used and shared with people that I mentor. Hopefully, some of these tools will help you on your journey as well.

You will find that I have deliberately kept the topic of Purpose near the end of the book, as I think most of us struggle to find that vs. goals that are specific and tangible.

What you will also see is that reading and learning are central to who I am.

These books have influenced me & I have extensively applied the learnings both as a person and a leader. I have shared many of the resources so that you can use them as well.

Who is this book for? For anyone wanting to pivot, grow and change. Though most of my experiences are from the vantage of a senior leader, it *can help anyone who thinks they are stuck professionally.*

Read and share back with me on sv_253@hotmail.com or https://www.linkedin.com/in/sandhya-vasudevan-2b14278/

1
THE TRANSITION: GOALS AND CURRENT REALITY

Self-Awareness for Evolving Career Goals and Recognizing your Current Reality

"What is PGROW?" you may ask.

If you're feeling stuck in a rut, experiencing dissatisfaction, or sensing a disconnect with your work, and you're longing to rediscover your professional purpose and need a compass to find your way forward, then my journey of transition will offer you some ideas for moving ahead.

Most transitions consist of a series of sprints until one finds the marathon they want to run. This process can take time — mine has taken over 30 months and is still evolving. Of course, if you're lucky, it can be just a few days, weeks, or months. Over the years, I've come to accept that this will be a process one needs to go through every time there's a serious pivot in their career. To regain a sense of control, I've utilized a very simple tool to help me navigate this journey — let's call it PGROW, or Professional Goal; Current Reality; Options; and Way Forward. I first encountered a variant of this process at Thomson Reuters and have adapted it for over 15+ years.

First, identify your immediate professional goals, assess your current reality, and understand and accept it, warts and all! Then, identify the gap between your current reality and your goal, then explore some options for moving ahead, and finally, select a path forward. Voila — PGROW!

Before starting the exercise, let me share a story of how I used it first: I was in Axa, and I had a new boss. My professional goal was to learn from him and deliver to the best of my ability. My reality was that he had been brought in after I had delivered a lot. As a director in the company explained, "S, you have broken a lot of eggs to deliver what you have. So even though you are more than capable of growing the organization, people may not positively support you". The new person had a lot to offer, yet I was used to a lot of freedom in the way I operated. The gap to the goal was that it no longer felt like it was my 'baby.' My options were to adjust and continue, OR look outside for another opportunity. I started with the first, I.e. adjust, but when a head-hunter reach out, I accept the new job.

Exercise:

If you want to take a few minutes to write down your professional goals and reality and see how you can refine them along with me, please do so. I believe that it can be a practical approach to managing change.

1. **Professional Goals**
   - ……………………………………….....
   - ………………………………………..…
   - ………………………………………..…

2. **Current Reality**
   - ………………………………………..…
   - ………………………………………..…

Let us now define immediate goals, their importance, and their purpose.

1. Immediate Goals

My professional goals were unclear, and my current reality was shaped by the aftermath of the first Covid wave and the passing of my father, leaving me emotionally drained and feeling "GREY."

Despite typically being enthusiastic about my work, this time, I seemed to have lost my mojo and simply wanted to move out of my current job.

When you are feeling 'GREY", PGROW can be a practical tool to try and shift from that state to a more desired outcome. Even the effort of shifting will give you a sense of control.

Every time I have changed jobs, it has been after a great deal of introspection. Either a new opportunity presented itself to me, or once I decided I wanted to move, something usually materialized long before I actually quit my job.

As a pragmatist, I always made sure to ensure financial security and maintain my existing relationships before making a move. However, this time it was different.

If you can recognize that you are in a blue funk and cannot see ahead, then seeking support to propel yourself into a more positive state is crucial. This is not easy, and in my case, the second wave of Covid meant I was still confined to my home.

I knew I needed to start looking into the future rather than continuing with the status quo, as I was not comfortable with it.

Despite it going against all my instincts of safety and security, my immediate goal was to unplug and then figure out my next move. To help navigate this transition, I put myself through a series of sprints.

The disruption I created for myself became the precursor to the opportunities that came my way.

I was in a crisis of meaning, searching for my path forward; this 'Agile' or iterative approach was a useful way to regain a sense of control over my life. *Agile is a methodology that involves breaking a project into phases and emphasizes continuous collaboration and improvement.*

2. Importance of Goals

Management and leadership emphasize the importance of goals and targets. Even books on manifesting, such as 'Secret,' [1]by Byrne Rhonda, speak about establishing clarity of purpose and consciously setting out to achieve it. Yet, in real life, we often set goals without the deliberate intention that we should accord them.

Most of us have a *vision* of our lives where we are happy and successful in all areas without much specificity. We may sporadically set *missions* that we chase, or we may be driven in some areas of our lives, but most of us don't deliberatively stay focused. We may have a wish or desire, yet we don't work to understand how to make it a reality. Most of us don't live intentionally. *With even a little focus, we can achieve a lot.*

As we finish our education, most of us want a job, and some want to become entrepreneurs. We may work to be the most effective in these roles. We also go after the next role, position, and wealth/knowledge that comes with it. We may get the impression that we are chasing a target, yet we are not always clear why we are chasing that particular dream.

3. Goal-Setting: Purposeful and Practical

Goal-setting and martial arts have a wonderful relationship. Master Shi Hen Yi, 35th generation Shaolin Master and Headmaster of the Temple of Europe in Germany[2], in one of his videos[3], shared his perspectives on this topic –first set the Goal and then start practicing, practicing, practicing. Sometimes, we achieve the Goal quickly; sometimes, it may take years or even decades! In that time, we learn to enjoy the journey and become masters of those arts. This 'Warrior's *mindset of one-pointed focus with attention on the here and now'* has always appealed to me. I was fortunate to learn judo in school, Karate when I was going through the Thomson Reuters merger, and in recent times, TaiChi / QiGong – *it was this meditative focus, coupled with action, which I found most attractive – Purposeful and Practical.*

As a friend of mine asked – why and how did this help you? Whether it is martial arts or golf, we set a goal and practice. With each practice, we analyze what needs to change, and we start becoming a witness to our actions. This approach spills into our work and other areas of our life.

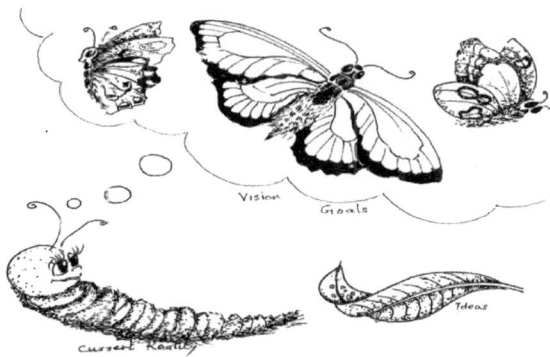

Yet, as I was leaving Deutsche, I had no clarity except the realization that I was no longer happy in my job -which meant that I did not have a goal. So, I decided to break this issue into bite-sized challenges or sprints. The first was to exit from Deutsche. Next was to identify my immediate next steps. This led me to a period of *Exploration*. Finally, based on what my explorations revealed to me, I started *consolidating my professional life into a coherent structure*. What does this look like? For me, I have a portfolio of activities such as independent directorship, working as a strategic consultant with start-ups and scale-ups, and contributing to a national think tank as a distinguished professor. For you, this could be to become a senior manager, a product leader, or a founder.

I am now in a steady state, and I will periodically review this against my shifting goals. As part of this exercise, I will add, drop, or change my construct until my next inflection point, when I will need to re-invent myself again.

Tools such as Ikigai *[there is more on this later in the chapter]* are great for understanding how one can frame goals. All I knew was that I had to find my new balance.

4. My Sprints to Move Ahead:

As I transitioned from my old life to a new career path, I carried out a series of sprints. I hope you find this experience of mine of value to you.

Sprint 1: Unplug from Current Reality

I won't go into details on how I finally exited Deutsche Bank [my current reality], but suffice it to say that it took over six months, with support from friends and well-wishers who ensured that this exit occurred smoothly. It was bitter-sweet as I had really enjoyed my stint with Deutsche. It has given me a lot of opportunities to learn and make friends. When we go through these transitions, some of the following might be helpful.

a. Ensure you have a Personal Board of Directors:

To ensure that my exit was smooth, I spoke to a host of friends, trusted colleagues, and mentors. I was validating my decision and, more importantly, asking for guidance on the best way to exit and start moving ahead into my next phase.

My circle of advisors includes family, professional, and personal friends. Let me share how Professor [Dr] Vasanthi Srinivasan became my trusted advisor. It was during the Thomson Reuters merger. I was the only one named in my role as country head, ...it was a fraught environment as both the Thomson and Reuters teams were not happy with the merger. The levels of trust were low, and that was when I met the professor for the first time. She was someone who had a dispassionate view of the situation, and she had empathy. She also wanted me to succeed. Though she was not close at that time, she was the best advisor.

Exercise:

Do you have this circle of trusted advisors?

1. If yes, list them ....

2. If no, what will you do to build your personal board of directors? ....

3. What action will you take to make this a reality?

Often, the best advisors may not be your family or friends. The family has your back as the whole YOU and not just professionally. Over the years, I have surrounded myself with a set of people with whom I consult on various professional matters. They are a mix of professional colleagues, friends, and family and may also include counselors and wellness experts. This sanity check will enable you to select your way forward in a balanced and pragmatic way without your internal states coming your way.

Remember, they provide perspectives, but *only WE decide*. If you do not have a set of advisors, then start building this now – it is never too late!

b. Practicality Matters!

When we are working, we have a financial plan, our professional networks, and our social volunteering activities in place. Yet when we are unplugging, especially without having an immediate next job, it is important to do a sense check on the mundane, such as do you need to change your bank accounts to get a handle on your long-term investments, which were handled by your employers; ensure you have professional networks even if you are no longer part of a company; do find places to volunteer which are not just part of your office community. Most importantly, have you updated your CV and got endorsements from people in your current organization when it is relatively easy to do so?

We also take a lot of infrastructural and organizational support for granted when we work for someone; here is the checklist that I used:

1. Personal laptop, printer, scanner, and other home office systems.
2. Tech and cybersecurity support
3. Admin and infrastructural support, many of these may have been in/ near your office – such vehicles, courier services, laundry pick, stationery items
4. Secretarial support
5. Formal professional networks

If not, be pragmatic and don't get stressed. Create your checklist and put them in place. What I miss most are the amazing assistants that I have had over my career, who made my life easy – yet now I share some support and have found AI assistants!

c. Saying goodbyes and getting your contacts updated

Appreciate and thank all those who have supported you, even if you didn't feel like doing so at that time. It is not just a polite thing, but it will uplift your mood to remember all those who helped you and meant well. This also enables you to keep the doors open for future interactions.

The final touch, for me, was a post on my LinkedIn for all those who had been part of my corporate journey. It was cathartic and truly freeing.

d. Permission to relax

Even if it is just binge-watching Netflix, playing a sport [I became serious about Yoga and Taiichi/ Qigong]; learning an instrument [I tried to learn the drums, and my teacher was so thankful when I finally dropped out!], take up art [Botanical Art was what helped me] ....and definitely spend time with your family, friends, and pets [these were my backbone].

Sprint 2: What next?

This sprint was more complex: My Goal was to understand my professional way ahead. For this, I had to understand my current Reality and envision the options ahead.

a. Impact of the World Around

The external world in early 2021 was the start of the *second wave of Covid*. It hit the world hard and devasted lives; the collective grief, fear, and depression engulfed millions across the globe. People were reeling from this experience, which was both global and personal.

The *great resignation was beginning*, and many serious professionals were stepping out of their careers to pursue more purposeful lives. Those who stayed with their organizations were concerned with job losses while supporting their colleagues through very stressful situations. The organizations were trying to survive, drive growth, and lead change, and the toll was on all the people.

The *virtual working and social isolation* made this period even more exhausting. Surviving and thriving took on a whole new meaning, and the way of judging careers was changing.

b. My professional Reality

At that time, I was a senior MD at Deutsche Bank, looking after Risk and governance with a global and regional remit. It was very interesting when I started in 2018. Yet this role constantly made us look at the under-belly of human nature.

We were focused on trying to prevent risk from manifesting, and this was exhausting. We were presenting our best efforts to the regulators, and this meant that even a simple document would be scrutinized by at least fifty to sixty people. All would review and critique it and tear it apart before it was signed off. This approach is truly stimulating during a growth phase or when building a product or driving innovation.

Yet it can be extremely draining when people are stressed and are constantly walking on eggshells due to internal and external pressures. After a certain point, our state of mind can make even the most exciting job exhausting and joyless. This is where I was professionally. After *35 years, I could not find my mojo at work!*

For me, this was very disturbing. I truly had no idea what to do next. The only thing I knew was that I needed to move in a different direction.

c. Change is a Choice

Change happens when one chooses it. Sometimes, we choose the change because of our internal state of mind. Yet, at other times, the external situation changes, and we need to embrace change, or else we cause collateral damage.

When we choose Change, then we subconsciously start scanning the horizon for anything that will help us on this journey. Opportunities come our way, and we sometimes don't recognize them; at other times, we don't accept them because of past conditioning; and sometimes, we seize the day! That is when magic happens.

For me, a chance lunch invite in January 2020 to a quasi-government/corporate event sparked off this journey. At this event, we shared what our companies were doing to support Covid and other social impact challenges. When it was my turn to speak, I did not want to focus on what my company was doing but chose to share some ideas that I was interested in. One of the ideas was that India should be putting a stake in the ground for Quantum Sciences. It is still a relatively new field, and I felt that there was potential for India to be in the circle of five within the next 25 years.

To my surprise, one of the Government/political officials reached out to me to get a whitepaper done. Not being a scientist, I reached out to a senior industry leader who was on the government's scientific panel, and we got some whitepapers out. It was also great, almost electric, to meet every Saturday morning to discuss amazing possibilities on how we could move ahead. Surprisingly, the document was passed by the state government, yet, like many things, it got morphed into something else.

This gave me a taste of what I was missing in my current role.

d. *Explore before Committing*

Often, to move ahead, we have to drop or at least distance ourselves from the current situation. Secondly, one needs to open oneself to new experiences, ideas, and possibilities. Otherwise, we will jump into the very same situation even in a new job! We need to recognize our patterns from our past to avoid them in the future.

While I still did not know my future professional goal, I knew that I had to de-couple all the baggage from the past and find the joy that I always had in my work. With this decision, despite the uncertainty, I felt a sense of freedom and relief, and it seemed as though I had a quest.

Anchor yourself in hope and have a support system to propel you forward.

Sprint 3: *Find your Ikigai*

Ikigai is a Japanese term that translates to "a reason to live." It helps you look at what you love to do in terms of what the world needs, what you are good at, and what you can be paid for. This can then become your mission, passion, profession, or vocation – i.e., your reason to live.

a. *My Reality – Another Perspective*

Working for multi-national companies in CXO roles, I was used to long work hours and deadlines. The hectic schedule did not give me enough time to engage outside with start-ups and NGOs on a personal level. I was also on the wrong side of 50 and knew that it would not be easy to find another senior role in an international organization *I had to take my first steps outside the corporate cocoon!*

There are two kinds of people: those who have clarity of who they are and what they intend to do when they leave a corporate career and others who are still wondering. I spoke to one person who had clarity. He had recently exited Oracle, and he had a clear sense of what he could offer. What he wanted was some tips and tricks to operationalize his goal for this phase of his career.

If you are like me, then you need to 'bake the goal' before moving forward. This meant that I had to approach goal-setting iteratively and in an agile fashion until the goal was found.

b. *Defining Professional Persona*

It is extremely difficult to define one's professional persona when one has no clarity. To the outside world, I had left the corporate career, and with no other job, I was a 'retired / jobless' person. It was galling. It made me mad since I did not see myself in that light. I still saw myself as an active professional who could contribute to strategy, provide operational support, and solve a problem for organizations. I saw myself as being part of organizations, even though I did not want to be a full-time employee. Yet, perception is reality, so I tried to pick myself up, spent time writing up my CV, and updated my LinkedIn – which had been virtually dormant for almost ten years. I decided to state that I was a Strategic Advisor and worked out an hourly / day rate for myself, apart from setting some vague financial goals. Today, I might have just called myself a professional explorer!

At this point, one of my bosses told me to get a job. Another suggested that I draw up what I wanted or didn't want in my next job. For example, in my next job, I may want to be clear that I did not want to travel for 150 days a year, even if I had done so in the past.

c. Guiding Principles

Over the years, every time I have established a goal, I have had some contours within which I operate. When I was younger, it was about quality of work and financial rewards. At other times, it included issues of values, for example, when I was joining the Guardian Royal Exchange. I told the person interviewing me that I would not fire people unless it was for ethical reasons, i.e., I was not comfortable with the 'hire and fire' approach.

At this time, my simple guiding principle was that *I must do what makes me feel positive. I also put down some practical guardrails.* As we were still in quasi-covid lockdown mode, I needed to be creative and manage this Exploration as remotely and virtually as possible.

The *Exploration phase* had a number of iterative activities: managing my day-to-day, setting up mini-projects / new experiences and volunteering, and finding a new job, or developing my 'consulting' opportunities; learning about the start-ups, learning through reading/listening to podcasts / YouTube and rebuild my network for the future. *They were activities and not really outcomes.*

If you just want to stay busy, interact with people. Activities are also good options. Driving outcomes are linked with being more intentional in what we want to achieve ...depending on your temperament, you can choose what works for you.

d. Living Day-to-Day

After 35 years of being a workaholic, I knew that I would be spooked by not having a strong set of daily deliverables. Hence, I created ongoing projects for myself – doing six events on Botanical Art and supporting the Cancer Institute, which I have been involved with for over 25 years, with Digital marketing. These projects involved volunteering; I also learned about building a community, running an art competition, and digital marketing.

I learned more through this experience than I might have if I had joined a formal program.

At the end of each day, I would tick off what I had done and plan my schedule for the next day/week. I had a rough plan for the next 3-6 months. It made me feel in control. These periods of uncertainty can easily zap your confidence.

e. Baby Steps into the future

At this time, I had also committed to *speaking at various forums* at least once a month for the next six months, including with Everywoman [4], which is an international organization supporting the cause of Diversity, Equity, and Inclusion.

I found the Harvard Business School 1-minute reads and various Neuroscientific hacks for improving productivity to be great tools to keep my spirits going.

The most energizing aspect was to *talk to people* about my mini-projects or what I was reading/listening to. The *enthusiasm and perspectives* that one share can be infectious, and it gets mirrored back to you from the person you are interacting with! I realized it was *my state of mind* that was getting *reflected back to me*!

f. Finding a job; setting up a consultancy or your own business:

A younger colleague of mine told me that my *digital presence* was abysmal, and I needed to *update my LinkedIn profile, set up my website,* and educate myself on how to *manage my digital persona.*

If you have been in corporate roles for a long time, you barely understand what one's *CV or bio-data* looks like. Often, it's not just the document but the emotions you attach to your experience that make it effective! So don't be afraid to experiment.

I went for a few *corporate interviews* as I was still not sure whether I wanted to exit the corporate world completely. The first interview was almost within a few days of leaving my job. It had been set up by a colleague of mine who had recently joined one of the big 4. The interview with the partners was a disaster! I was still in my senior MD mode and was not in any frame of mind to move ahead. I suspect the partner did not enjoy that meeting either! The second opportunity was interesting, and in NY, but it was not for me. As time went by, I realized that I no longer wanted the corporate roles, and I had been self-sabotaging myself at the meetings!

Throughout my career, I served as a director *on various boards*, and when I left, I felt a sense of freedom from that responsibility. Yet I had good friends and colleagues telling me that I should become an independent director. So, I went for some of these discussions. They did not work out. I don't know how much was self-sabotage again and how much was truly a mismatch. Yet, it is important to explore possibilities, even when we don't want to do so. I reached a point where I consciously stayed away from non-executive director roles until about a year or so later when I embraced independent directorships. Explore and see what fits you!

g. Practical tips for job-hunts and independent directorships

Maintain relationships with HR professionals who can help you with your career.

They may be recruiting firms and HR professionals in companies where you are interested in joining. Also, talk to people in your network about what you have done and are interested in doing. Virtually all my opportunities came from my network.

Today, this is my Ikigai – as it leverages my competence, it is what the company and the larger ecosystem need, and there is a board fee.

h. Strategic Consulting

I tried my hand at *strategic consulting*, and it *was truly enjoyable*. My best experience was seeing a team working on a humanoid robot and another on cybersecurity.

Not all opportunities convert into revenue – yet all provide learning opportunities and insights. A visioning exercise with a non-banking financial company unexpectedly turned into an Independent Director role.

Be enthusiastic and engaged in your explorations. Some will convert into unplanned opportunities, while others will bring you friends!

i. Entering and Contributing to the Start-up ecosystem

Given today's environment, the start-up ecosystem is most

vibrant and inviting. A good friend of mine told me that it is a highly chaotic environment, and after a structured bank career, it would take some time to get used to. So, it made me curious, yet diffident, about how to contribute to this ecosystem.

At this time, as part of the Young President's Organizaton, I came across an Entrepreneurship program with a business school, and I joined it for the new networks as well as to replace my banking perspective with a start-up mindset. I was the grandmother of my class, but it was great getting back into learning.

I also joined the Masterclass with the Indian Angel Network. Shortly after that, I became a member of The Indus Entrepreneurs [TiE], which is a global organization supporting start-ups with Chapters in over 65 cities across the globe.

I then went to meet some of my connections at the Indian Institute of Management, Bangalore's NSRCEL, and after a couple of conversations, I formally became a mentor at their start-up cell.

I also attended a Singularity University program with a focus on future technological changes. I started actively volunteering to evaluate start-ups, interview and short-list them for cohorts, and mentor them, apart from assessing them for investments with the Angel investing forums that I had joined. While I knew that I didn't want to be an entrepreneur, I certainly wanted to contribute to the ecosystem.

Here are some learnings from an investor's perspective for anyone wanting to become a founder.

    i. *Identify a problem or opportunity* that you are passionate about.

    ii. *Find a unique solution with a hurdle rate* that is difficult for others to replicate.

    iii. Ensure that this *solution creates value for as many stakeholders* as possible.

    iv. Make sure that you have a very *solid understanding* of your *financials and customers*.

    v. Find out who can provide you with advice and connections for both *sales* and *funding*.

vi. As an investor, I want to know that there is a *strong founding team* as well as a *strong business*.

vii. Understand the *legal and regulatory* aspects of your business as well as the *technology required*.

viii. *If you have a risk appetite, go for it. Be pragmatic about what you can financially handle.*

j. Leaning and re-inventing

When one is out exploring, people will reach out. An Israeli start-up reached out to me, and soon, I became their Strategic Advisor for a year or so. It was the most insightful and enjoyable experience. The culture of rigor, research orientation, and discipline was exactly what I liked. Finding kindred spirits was equally satisfying. Meeting the 93-year-old investor gave me a sense of possibilities – and how not to limit oneself. It exposed me to global gig workers and blockchain, as well as a pivot into the circular economy. Ultimately, I also found a good professional friend.

There are a number of other founders of start-ups with whom I have forged a strong relationship. They have all enriched me in ways I can never repay.

While I was talking to people, I also kept on listening to podcasts/YouTube sessions, and if they referred to somebody, sometimes I would go to LinkedIn and ping for a short conversation. One of them was Dr Rama Jayasundar, who is a nuclear magnetic resonance specialist and an Ayurvedic doctor. Though it was a very short conversation, she provided me with the perspective to understand the complex field of medicine through a very different lens [5]. This also got me talking to a number of Ayurvedic doctors and start-ups in this field.

I found a kindred spirit in Cambridge, Dr. Madan Thangavelu, who is doing amazing work. The conversations were far-reaching and extremely enriching, and they helped me distance myself from my old banking, risk, and regulatory mindset. Learning something new will definitely shift one forward in unintended directions.

k. Techniques to address the Gap between future aspirations and your existing education and experience –

especially if not aligned

i. *Develop Competencies*

A senior cloud services leader shared her story of how she was able to pivot to being a 'Cloud' specialist. During the lockdown, she joined a program on Cloud, and every morning after she completed a lesson, she wrote a blog on what she had learned. This not only helped her internalize her knowledge but also got others to see her as a leader in this field.

Another approach is to *find a place where one's relevance is naturally acknowledged*. Example: I am interested in medicine, especially integrative/holistic healthcare. Yet when I shared this interest with someone, they said that I wouldn't be taken seriously because I am not from the healthcare field. Yet *I am a potential 'customer'* either as a patient or caregiver and hence have every right to shape the Healthcare ecosystem. Do not allow others to tell you what you can or cannot do. This is what the Patient for Patient Safety Foundation [6] does.

A third approach is to *find an adjacency*. When I became the FinTech Chair for TiE Bengaluru, I leveraged my 35 years of financial services and tech experience, including working with start-ups.

Finally, *try new things if you get even the smallest opportunity*. It may not work out, but it will open other doors. An ex-colleague of mine from NY wanted us to try a consulting gig ... we actively explored and met some people. It did not work out, but we had fun, and most importantly, it gave me new ideas to progress. I have been roped in as a Champion for IP and Quantum due to my enthusiasm. When things are changing, friends are welcome!

ii. *Network Building*

Exploration is easier in one's imagination than in Reality. Hence, turn to your networks. I realized that my *professional networks* of over 25+ years were mainly based on the organizations I worked for and my industry peers. My *personal relationships* and competence may have enabled me to be active in these forums, but many of these networks only have *organizational membership*. So, it is important to find spaces where *individual memberships* are possible. I had set this up earlier in my career, and I also *set up an LLP to enable me to join the business forums, where only institutional memberships are accepted.*

With this in place, I told myself that I would *talk to at least 100* people within the next six months. I identified people from 10-20 years back with whom I had had a good relationship. I found people on LinkedIn and asked for a meeting, or after a virtual conference, I would ask for a short discussion. For example, I was at a virtual fire-side chat that was being hosted by an ex-colleague of mine from Thomson Reuters. We had not met for over 15 years, yet she set me up with a meeting with the author she had been interviewing. *He was Marcus Greenberg, who had written the book The Primitives. Disparate experience. He speaks about those who follow their own path. For example, a lady who was a zoo keeper, a New York reporter, and then became the right-hand person for Mayor Bloomberg.*

This meeting gave me a sense of validation for the journey that I was on! A stranger is a mirror without your bias.

My guidelines for networking were to *talk to people, say yes to* as many *opportunities* that come my way as a result of these conversations, *say no to Boards* and anything that constraints my explorations, and *accept when people say NO* to me – i.e., grow a thick skin.

My learnings from these conversations were truly amazing, and maybe one day, I will share the *wisdom from friends*! I found talking about my projects opened up avenues for further discussions. Asking about people's journey and their ideas on what I could do was fascinating. One of my ex-bosses wanted me to find a job quickly as she felt that I would go off my career track. Others wanted me to stay put in my job as I still had a few years left for retirement.

    iii.   Creating a Professional Portfolio

Yet others spoke about new possibilities and *creating a portfolio of activities* that I enjoyed – the best of this advice came from Ravi Venkatesan, who had just written: "What the Heck do I do with my Life." [7]

At the end of one year, I realized I had a completely new network.

I connected with people from small and big towns in India and people from different parts of the world who are involved in start-ups, consulting, and ESG [Environmental, Social, and Governance]. Each of these conversations gave me a new perspective on the world.

What was clear to me was that I did not need to take a traditional path, and I didn't need to do what others said I should. I needed to listen, understand, and create my own mind map!

Sprint 4: To Consolidate Professional Activities, My New Reality:

At the end of the first year, I had still not landed on what I wanted to do, but I found myself active in the start-up sector. I was a member of The Indus Entrepreneurs [TiE Bengaluru]. I became a mentor with IIMB NSRCEL, which was well-recognized. I was a member of the Angel network forum and was often engaged in the evaluation of start-ups. I was a member of Social Venture Partners, and I joined 2 of their Fast Pitch programs to help select and support the short-listed founders to get funding. I was also engaged with a national think tank, looking at education, the future development of the country, the creator economy, and even Quantum! I realized that I liked the portfolio approach to my career. It gave me the flexibility and excitement that came from variety.

After fifteen months, I knew that I was now ready to join boards, especially if they aligned with my areas of interest, growth, change/transformation, and inclusive growth/impact and enabled me to learn new things.

Finally, I arrived at an internal guiding principle on what I would work on: "Creation of Abundance – whether for the society, company, founder or myself." It became easier to say NO to things that did not fit into this construct.

In the Start-up ecosystem, we are often presented with an opportunity. Do we recognize it? Do we say yes to it? Here are a few where I said yes and consolidated my engagement in this area.

I took up the responsibility of TiE Bengaluru Governance Board and FinTech Chair.

I proactively engaged and became a nominee director on behalf of the Angel community with a start-up.

I also became more selective in my engagements with the start-ups.

Once I said yes to becoming an Independent Director, I found opportunities coming my way. I needed to ensure that I was qualified despite having the experience. I picked only those boards where I was sure that my risk appetite was aligned with the company and that I had trusted references before joining.

This is an area that I am actively enjoying, and with many, I offer more than just board engagement.

Within Social Venture Partners [8], I joined their grants and partnership committee. As a banker, I know a lot of people in the ecosystem, but as part of a social venture, the relationships and engagements are different, and this is definitely a new territory.

Lastly, my engagement with the national think tank has morphed into one where I am a board member as well as a Distinguished Professor.

During this phase, I got involved with inputs for the national education policy, ideas for development for the next 25 years for the country, and a champion for Intellectual property.

Tools and Takeaways:

While I continued to use *my very basic tool of PGROW*, I was also leveraging other tools such as:

- *The Four-Hour WorkWeek by Timothy Ferriss [9]*
- *The LifeBook by Jon and Missy Butcher [10]*
- Japanese concept of *Ikigai [11]*

which has become popular in recent years. Let me share how I used them. You can find more material on their websites.

The Four-Hour Workweek templates are available for you to plan your future.

I customized these templates to fit my needs into three basic questions over the next 6 months to 3 years or more:

Exercise:
Within 6 months and 3 years
1. What do I want to Do? ....
2. What do I want to Have? and ....
3. What do I want to Be? ....

When I read the book, what struck me was that we think we want something, but in reality, we just want an experience. For, there are a number of companies offering to time-share properties in wonderful holiday destinations. We can enjoy the holidays in those places, but we do not need to own the holiday homes. I used this thought process in 2010 before I moved to Deutsche Bank from Thomson Reuters. It enabled me to build clarity around what experiences I wanted vs. what I really needed to own. It helped me make a number of decisions – such as living a commuting lifestyle and living in a hotel vs. owning a second home in another city.

The Lifebook by Missy and Jon Butcher is a tool I came across many years ago. You can find this tool in MindValley [12]. Lifebook makes one take a look at 12 areas of life: Health and Fitness, Intellectual Life, Emotional Life, Spiritual Life, Character, Career [*professional*], Financial Life, Love Relationship, Social Life, Parenting [*Family*], and Quality of Life and Life Vision. Like most goal-setting tools, it makes you set your Vision and your Strategic Plan – this is defined through 4 buckets:

- Premise [What do you believe?],
- Vision [What do you want?],
- Purpose [Why do I want it?],
- Strategy [What can I do to achieve it?].

What LifeBook does differently is that it asks you to *identify your beliefs* in these areas and the *reason WHY these goals are important* for you. The underlying factors can be your roadblocks or enablers in achieving your goals. It made back into the underlying philosophies that drive my life. This is also a highly iterative process, and many people work on a few areas at a time. What is most important is to recognize that each area has an impact on the other.

Professionally, I was not geared to be a lotus eater.

Partly, this came from my family role models, where *my father and grandfather worked into their 80s, and my mother is the same.* This meant that I was not geared for a lotus-eater life. Secondly, I was *driven by my learning needs* and not necessarily financial returns. This was a double-edged sword, and after much introspection, it helped me evolve my approach to what I now do: *Support the development of Abundance.* For pure social initiatives, I don't charge; for start-ups, I charge a reasonable rate; and for commercial operations, it is the market rate.

I need to frame what I am doing as part of something bigger than myself.

Examples

My role as the Chair of TiE FinTech Special Interest Group [SIG], where in partnership with the state [Karnataka Digital Economy Mission], we are supporting the aspiration of the state to become a $300 billion digital economy by 2028.

Being involved with the national think-tank to look for initiatives that impact the long-term development of the country through seminars and papers and being a champion for different initiatives such as IP for Quantum.

Joining foundations is involved in development. For example, Industree is focused on developing livelihoods for women through the field of crafts for the marketplace or Social Venture Partners.

5. Connecting to the Creative Side

Finally, during this period, I was connecting to my creative side. In the past 35 years, I have been immersed in the financial and tech sector, which has leveraged my analytical side. Now, I find myself mentoring founders in the creative space – for example, the CEO of Match My Talent [13], who has created a database of performing artists and has run a number of virtual film festivals [14]. I also make time to do some art.

These explorations made me acknowledge ***the Ikigai*** *as a central tool for my change.* These introspections made me aware that I am very effective at linking up very random bits of data and providing perspective, ideas, and differentiated solutions. I remember during a senior leadership psychological assessment in 2000 at a Maidstone assessment center, my ability to correlate was in the top 15% of the top 15%. I am finally finding ways to actively leverage capability in a way that I enjoy, and it benefits others. I have found institutions that value this type of cross-disciplinary perspective and my ability to connect unplanned dots. I realized that some of my goals, in Ikigai terms, will be part of my 'mission,' which seems to have resonated with my engagement with the think tank. While not remunerative, it gives me immense joy.

Check out what makes you unique and how does it affect your choices. It is possible that what you Love to do today may not be what the market wants, so could you work on making this goal a reality? A good friend of mine, a banker, decided she wanted to be a healer. She started training herself as a psychologist, a hypnotherapist, and in other alternate methods of healing. It was not an easy pivot, but it was resoundingly fulfilling.

This Exploration made me review one of my old goals, which was to read the complete works of Shakespeare. I used to read King Lear to my grandfather. At that time, this goal was very important – firstly, it gave me a way to hang out with my grandfather. Secondly, as a student, I was told that Shakespeare had amazing insights into the human psyche and that it is relevant even today. Yet, after 30 years of professional experience, I have a fair understanding of human nature, so reading Shakespeare is more of self-indulgence. Today, I have recast this goal to 'read more about the latest technology' - *I want to learn* about DeepTech as it is *more relevant*!

These tools gave me the framework to explore my professional journey. PGROW is a simple tool that reduces complexity in addressing a problem. The Four-Hour Workweek and the LifeBook gave more depth to my explorations. A major takeaway from these was to identify my Goals/issues and accept my current Reality. Once we accept our current Reality, the *Options open up to create our New Reality!*

Takeaways

1. ***Our journeys are iterative***, and we *need to be agile*; hence, *micro-goals* are important; *mindset is vital*; finding and *creating solutions* is essential.

2. **Build a warrior's mindset**- Focused and one-pointed.

3. The **sub-goals with multiple sprints** help us manage our transition with greater ease and a sense of control.

4. **Getting buy-in from stakeholders**: I worked on a proposal that got interest from a primary stakeholder, yet to operationalize it, I had to find ways to get buy-in from various other players. This can sometimes be time-consuming. During a visioning exercise, we had to get over 30 of the leaders aligned, and it did not seem that all of them got the message. Yet a year later, even the laggards were owning the Vision. This type of effort is very complex when engaging with ecosystem changes.

5. **Selfcare:** During this journey, *self-care is vital*, be it *exercise, sleep, nutrition, mental and physical well-being.* Life is going to throw challenges; there could be internal and external factors that will impact your trajectory. If you are at your physical and mental best, you will have resilience.

6. **Social circle.** There is significant research showing the importance of social interaction for one's mental well-being. My mother, who's 84, has an immediate social circle that is probably better than mine. She tries to go out and engage with them almost every day. Establish those support systems when you're at your best or in the most comfortable state. This investment will definitely play a major role when you need it. Professionally find people who have achieved or working to achieve similar goals to yours; this will help you in many ways – subtle competition, collaboration, supportive group...

Exercise:

1. Review your notes on the PGROW, which you wrote down for yourself. See if you want to make any changes to what you have written.

2. -Professional goal ....

3. -Current Reality ....
4. Gap to Goal.................................
5. Options to achieve the goal by bridging the gap...............
6. Way Forward ....[next steps]

6. Gender Perspective of Career Choices

A number of years ago, Professor Vasanthi Srinivasan [Indian Institute of Management, Bangalore] spoke about the gender identities of women and how that impacts careers. At that time, the research showed that most women did not own their *professional identity as a primary identity*. At the same time, men, in their breadwinner role, had the professional persona as a primary identity.

The world is changing, and we are seeing significant *shifts in gender* roles. In the family unit, where both partners are educated, and often both have careers/jobs, the couple makes decisions as a unit and not as male or female.

One of the guys who worked for me moved to the US without a job when his partner got a promotion to NY, while another chose not to take a lucrative opportunity since both the partners were highly successful in their jobs, and the new role, with re-location of one of the partners, would upset their delicate childcare set-up.

7. Our professional lives do not exist in a vacuum.

I remember when I fell *seriously ill* earlier in my career, I needed to put myself first, definitely ahead of my job. When my dad fell ill, the *elder care* made me rescript the way I went about my life, including my career. You may have *child care*, or your *partner may need support* as they may be moving to another country with a promotion – we all need to evaluate what makes sense for us at that time.

You may have *financial challenges*, which makes you look at your job with a different lens. All of these factors will impact the choices you make for your career.

We will examine the impact of these factors on your professional journey in the next chapter.

2
YOU ARE MORE THAN YOUR CAREER!

Implications of Competing Life Goals

1. Unexpected Always Happens!

In the previous chapter, clarity of professional aspiration was established, but this is not enough!

-I had a dream job with Guardian Royal Exchange in a new industry, with inspiring people, when I was unexpectedly diagnosed with a serious illness.

-One of my team was selected to be a team manager, and he was slated to spend a few months in the UK as part of this transition. It was a great career opportunity. Then he got the news that his father was terminally ill, and he had to choose between his career and his family.

-A banker friend of mine found her passion to become a holistic healer. From being a well-paid banker, she was starting afresh in a field where there was no guarantee that she would be successful.

-A young researcher friend of mine was offered a job in one of the top pharma companies in Switzerland.

From a junior academician in a small university in India, he became part of a premier global R and D lab!

Our professions do not operate in a vacuum. There are many dimensions in our lives, and they all impact each other. Life is about balancing our different needs and aspirations, and they will dynamically change from time to time. The changes could be your role in the family, or your mental and physical health, your financial needs and wealth goals, and your societal and community aspirations. They could either aid your professional goals or be out of alignment with them. In this chapter, we will explore the implications of competing goals and our approaches to handling them in the context of our profession.

I will focus significantly on the Financial and Wealth creation goals as they are closely aligned with our Careers. I will also touch on the other goals, though not to the same extent.

2. Insight into Self-Awareness

The journey of Self-awareness can be an amazing goal in and of itself. It is an ongoing process, and if we examine each experience with this mindset, it can be fun while providing great insight!

My last corporate role was definitely a *balancing act between being professionally relevant* and *elder care*. When my father fell ill and was no longer able to fully manage his health needs on his own, I knew I had to make changes in the way I lived.

It was as though a huge tree was in the process of getting

uprooted, and I was trying my puny best to keep it up.

It meant that I could no longer go off around the world, working all hours. I had to take a hard call, and I was fortunate to find a significant role, though very different from what I would have normally chosen. It was interesting while enabling me to take into consideration the home needs.

When I was switching into this role, my boss was very understanding and spoke about the *values by which I was operating; for me, it was a choice from the heart.* Settling into that role, I actively dropped out of most social activities, including professional forums and networking events. My priorities were elder care, work, and self.

With the advent of Covid, most professionals become more people-centric, whether at work, with family, or with friends, through family friends' video calls and office colleagues sharing personal details.

The homes became offices! It was also a time of intense personal introspection. Many were going through this, including me. Often, acquaintance would share their thoughts on what their career should look like going forward.

Long back, when Guardian Royal Exchange' bought PPP Healthcare, a number of senior insurance colleagues from Guardian Health left the company and moved into completely different professions. The most interesting ones were someone becoming a landscape designer and another a pilot for short hops across the country. I don't know whether it was to explore their passion or if they were just waiting for their next professional opportunity during their garden leave. It made me realize that careers don't need to be linear or follow a trodden path, especially when I saw that many went back to bigger and better roles in the industry.

3. Competing and Enhancing Life Goals
a. *Financial and Wealth Goals*
i. *Financial Goals and Current Reality*

The first time I became aware that I needed to save for the future was when I was in my early 30s. I had savings and thought it was more than enough to live forever! By today's standards, it would have lasted a couple of years!

The importance of wealth creation became clear to me when, during a job offer, I was asked to share my wealth goals. They wanted to offer shares in lieu of the salary that I was getting. It was the first time I had to think through planning for my long-term wealth creation. I decided to stay in my job – 'bird in hand vs. two in a bush.' Maybe I should have taken the shares!

If you are changing your career, whether it's a job, moving to be an entrepreneur, or just following your passion. *It is important to be pragmatic about one's financial situation.* If you are young and don't have family responsibilities, then you can definitely take risks and explore, as the consequences are just for you. Yet if you have a family who needs your financial contribution or if you have active financial goals to buy a house/car/ study, then this would be an important consideration in your decision-making.

Recently, a young entrepreneur who was just becoming successful also got her dream spot in an Ivy League college – *competing opportunities:* one where immediate financial benefits are visible and the other where long-term opportunities exist. She was excited about both, but as the time grew closer to joining college, her dilemma about her start-up was intense – does she shut it down, keep it going remotely with help, sell it. It was both a financial and an emotional decision. No right answers! What would you do in this situation?

I tend to turn to books -Wealth is one of the fundamental elements for living one's life, yet we don't always have clarity on our relationship with money. I have shared some of the books that helped me build a better understanding of this topic in the Resource section.

It is still a work in progress for me to see how financial well-being is affected by different aspects of my life.

ii. *Financial acumen is a learned skill!*

Recently, I was interviewed by a documentary filmmaker who asked me what advice I had for artists who focused on their creativity and did not want to be bogged down by all the mundane financial matters. I used the metaphor of health. Most of us would love to eat whatever we wanted. Yet, for health or other reasons, we try to eat right. Even if one does not want to do so, life insurance expects it of you! Financial prudence is no different. *Even if you are not good at managing money, you need to learn basic life skills.*

Coming from a defense family, I saw up-close what happens when the soldier dies, and the family struggles to survive.

Even with pensions, all the privileges that the family took for granted go away, and things like a good school, higher education, etc., all become challenging. It is *essential* for the partner *to be financially competent to manage life.*

Do you know what kind of life you want? Do you have that life right now? In financial terms, what will this look like? A friend of mine wanted to retire in the hills and grow fruits. She was living in Delhi with a great job and a young child. As a family, they started scouting for land in the hills, getting a house built, and slowly spending holidays out there. This also meant a second mortgage and longer hours at work! Yet it's a choice you make – view it as an investment or a pain!

iii. *Financial Independence and Financial Goals*

Is Financial Independence the same as your financial goal? Have you defined *what financial independence will look like?* Here are some scenarios. I can live for 3 years on my savings. I have enough to start a business. I have enough money to buy a property from which I can get rent. I have enough to send my child to college. I can travel around the world in comfort. I have put away enough pension funds to get a regular income when I retire. I have enough money to buy a plane, a houseboat, or an electric guitar. While insurance agents/accountants or maybe your family have a view on how much money you need to have, *only you can define what this amount is for yourself.* Think about this. It is important to have an emotional sense of *Financial Freedom. It is as much a mindset as a real number.*

When I was asked about my aspirations for wealth, I was confused. What did that mean? Growing up in a family of government servants, the mindset was to save for a comfortable retirement., i.e., save for a rainy day. In today's world, it is important to think about the material goals in conjunction with *your risk appetite*. If you join a start-up and it fails, you can chalk it up to experience, yet if it succeeds, then you may become very affluent. Your risk appetite will be based on your personality but also other factors, such as if you are the sole earning member or if your partner financially supports you? Or do you have other financial commitments that might be impacted if you do not have a certain money flow every month? Even if you are financially capable of taking the risk, do you have other pressures of child or elder care? *It's all about mindset.*

As I started earning, a pragmatic friend of mine said, "Buy a house and a second one for the rental income." Another opinion was that rental incomes are not much but have a pension income. What matters is, *will that particular approach give you peace of mind?*

To arrive at my *Financial Independence goal* was a process of exploration. I needed to understand my relationship with money. Most of us never understand it, but it is worth the effort as it helps you arrive at your point of financial freedom. I know my grandfather was meticulous at accounting for every expense. With 6 children, he wanted to be as prudent and effective with what he had. My father had this trait of carefully writing down his expenses and savings, but he had no real sense of wealth creation.

A good friend of mine, who comes from an entrepreneurial family, has a natural ease with which he works on wealth creation. He was talking to a bunch of college students and shared how his family supported entrepreneurship – if the young entrepreneur in the family failed, the family would pawn their things and give the bridge amount until they could turn the business around. Our hidden thoughts and beliefs in this area are significant, and they will impact your professional decisions.

One of my ex-CEOs always used to say that she liked her salespeople to aspire for nicer apartments, cars, and sailing boats. The rationale was that the sales folk who need money to buy these things will drive sales to make the commission to achieve their financial goal. Now, if a person believed in living a frugal life, would they really chase sales? Or maybe the question is, will the commission be a motivator?

At a certain point in our jobs, we all get disenchanted. We want to follow our passion, go work in the forest, or make a pledge to give 50% of our wealth as part of *Living My Promise* [1] or work with conservation or other social sector initiatives. Yet, as a good friend of mine said, I want to do all that, but I love my jet-setting lifestyle and living in 5-star hotels, which my job provides. So, what drives you?

Ultimately, knowing what your financial goals are and evaluating your current reality will have a strong impact on your professional choices. For me, Ikigai, with financial freedom, is central to my life's journey. When I was in college, earning a salary was financial freedom; as I grew older, it was about having enough to lead a comfortable life, and still, later, it became other life needs such as wealth-creation for children or elder care or your medical needs.

What you need to define is what financial freedom means for you. It is not about whether what you are doing has financial value for others.

When we feel a sense of financial freedom, that is when we can become Don Quixote without stress. That would be your passion or mission, definitely not your profession or vocation!

Choosing between financial goals and professional goals is tough. Ideally, it should be complimentary. Yet there are other tougher choices ahead! Before getting to the next section, why don't you take a few minutes to do the following exercise?

Exercise:

    Define these as specific, measurable, actionable, and time-bound terms

1. *Write down your Purpose or Goal around*
    i. Finance .... *[E.g. I need enough money to have a house by, and go on two holidays every year, buy branded clothes for the children, have elder-care support]*
    ii. Wealth........*[E.g. I need to create a corpus of $x by the time I am 35,*

have a debt-free house by age x or have a monthly income of $xxx when I retire]
2. What are your beliefs around money & wealth, and which of these beliefs impact your financial and wealth goals?
    i. Hinder......[E.g. thinking about money is not good; doubt & fear of success/ change/ rejection...; habit of resistance; family blocks; clashing values.....]
    ii. Support growth......[E.g. money can be used for good; mindset of abundance]
3. Why are these goals important......
4. Using PGROW, based on your financial goals
    i. What is your current reality...................................
    ii. What is the gap between current reality and financial goals ....
    iii. What are some of the options to bridge this gap...............
5. How does the financial goal impact your career goals ....[E.g. I want to become a start-up founder, but I have 2 college-going children who need financial support – do you wait until your financial commitment to your children is met, or do you get a student loan for them?]
    While I try to avoid examples in the exercises, I thought this topic merited them due to how we all respond to the topic of money.

   b. Relationships: Family, Friends, Professional colleagues
      i. Independent vs. co-dependent relationships

You have just got the most fantastic role, and your partner also has received a promotion, and both are in two different cities or continents. Your child needs special attention. If you uproot her, there will be significant turmoil. What do you do? It is no longer an individual decision. *A family unit will often need to establish co-dependent decision-making processes.* Tough one!

As a kid from an army background, this was a routine situation. The postings would arrive in the middle of the school year or when the child is in the 10 or 12 grade. In my family, the decision was prioritized based on the child's needs. In other situations, we may accommodate based on spouses' and elder care needs.

Often, we make decisions after getting the family's opinions, but ultimately, it is our decision, and it need not be a co-dependent decision. When I was leaving Thomson Reuters, a lot of my professional colleagues expected me to become an entrepreneur. My Dad was very uncomfortable with this option, as he felt it would jeopardize my financial security. As I did not have a burning passion for becoming an entrepreneur, it was easy to choose another corporate role. Here, it was an independent choice while accommodating another's concern.

ii. *Prioritizing Relationships*

During the Thomson Reuters merger, one of my biggest learnings was that, sometimes, if one cannot have a win-win outcome, then it is better to go with a lose-lose outcome than with a win-lose decision. During the merger, we had to pick a way to compensate new joiners into the company. The choice was whether we should pay a very high starting salary and then keep the annual increments reasonable or start with a reasonable salary with good increases year-on-year. Each team viewed their approach as being superior. So, we tried to find a third way so that neither team felt that they had won. If we had picked one approach over the other, we would have had one group feeling like the loser. This can affect relationships consciously or unconsciously.

iii. *Relationships define and influence goals.*

Defining goals in the context of your partner, your family/friends is important. Let us explore what some of these can look like.

A close relative of mine had a very strong commitment to his spouse, and that relationship took precedence over all other relationships. He had clearly established a priority of relationships. So even when his child wanted to share something exclusively with him, he would share it with his wife. The same was true with the other family members. The result was that all other relationships became secondary. This type of loyalty will impact one's professional choices. The partner may actively support a promotion or you becoming an entrepreneur or an artist, or they may not. While you accept the decision, if it is against what you want, will you resent it later? Something to evaluate honestly.

A colleague shared with me that she and her husband had a clear understanding that in the case of elder care, each of them would handle their parents with minimal support from the partner. This also could affect the professional space when both were dealing with their elders.

I had the following realization: When you hear the story, it will seem self-evident, and you will say, "Duh! It is obvious!" Yet I was blind to it. Having a successful career at a senior level meant that I rarely had time for my family and relatives. My cousins are very close to me, and I am very fond of them.

A few years ago, when we were planning a family holiday, we had a call to sync up the plans.

I joined late and heard one of my cousins say, "Don't ask S, she won't have the time to take it up."

It was very factual, but within the family group, it was clear that I had prioritized my career. It hit me that people who mean so much to me knew that I did not put them first.

If you want to be the fulcrum of your friends and family, the 'go-to' person, you may want to think about how to balance between family and profession.

Some people are fantastic at doing this, yet I had to consciously try to work on the individual relationships even though I was never going to be the "go-to" person.

iv. Create Relationship maps!

Stakeholder Management is not just for Project Management! As we **identify the key people in our lives,** we can use our own version of a *'stakeholder map'* [2] or, in this case, a relationship map. In a Stakeholder map, we typically look at how engaged they are with us and how influential they are in what we need to accomplish.

In the context of a *Relationship map*, I would use the following:

1. *How important is this relationship?*
2. What are some of the *guiding principles by which I operate?*
3. What do you want to do to *nurture the relationship?*

While one can draw this up, it is not easy to follow through, and it often comes with unintended consequences.

v. *Relationships transition over time.*

As a young person, I idealized my Dad. As I grew older, I realized that he was not perfect, and by the time I was in my mid-30s, I realized that he had 'wisdom'! So, one of my favorite activities for years was walking with my Dad and talking about my professional dilemmas. As a defense doctor, he often had no clue about how companies operated, but he was very interested, and I found a way to share my world with him. His life as a soldier and doctor often gave me unique perspectives, and he was definitely an ally who only wanted the best for me. At a senior level, we are often alone, and this kind of relationship is truly a blessing. Generally, we hold our child, partner, and parents as vital relationships, and we want to be there for them, but professionally, we are too busy, and as time goes by, the close relationships no longer expect much from you. At a later date, when we become aware of this distance and we want to rectify it, it takes a lot more effort. I was fortunate to have found a way to bridge that gap through a lot of personal investment in time.

Personal Board of Directors: I have been part of a business forum, Young President's Organization, since 2004. The small group has been meeting every month with semi-annual retreats over the years. While predominantly professional, we also discussed and shared about our families, self, and community activities. This unique group of people has been given priority in my life even when things have been tough. They are an important group within my relationship matrix. *Do you have your own 'Board of Directors'?* They could be even your mentors, life coaches, friends, family, or therapists.

vi. *Hidden baggage in our Relationships*

What makes us tick? What are the hidden beliefs that drive our behavior?

I come from a family that is not given too much physical display of affection. A pat on the shoulder or arm is deemed a major show of affection.

I remember during a fairly acrimonious situation at the office, after a lot of discussions, our boss asked me and my colleague to hug and make up. I was horrified! It might have been better for all if I had not reacted so much.

As the title of this chapter says, "You are more than your career." Let's **explore your relationships in the context of your professional journey.** At different stages in our lives, we will have various conscious and unconscious elements come through and affect us in what we choose and how we operate.

Relationships are fundamental, and workplaces have people with whom we need to build connections. With your boss, it's a co-dependent approach to decision-making; with your colleagues and subordinates, it's a consultative approach, and each of these will have a degree of prioritization. As you observe your personal relationships, you may get cues on how this translates into the workplace.

It is not just about aligning purposes but also about how we engage.

Exercise:
1. *Identify your Key Relationships...*
2. *Draw up a Relationship Map ....*
    i. *Priority of that relationship ...[e.g Child first, then ....].....*
    ii. *Guiding principles by which you operate in the relationship....*
    iii. *Practical actions that govern your relationship [e.g., call home twice].........*
3. *What are the beliefs around Relationships.......................*
4. *Those beliefs that hinder or ....*
5. *Beliefs that support growth..*
6. *Why are these goals important?...........................*
7. *Gap between your current state and relationship goals ....*
8. *How does it affect your goals for your career.....................*

   c. Self: Physical, mental, emotional, spiritual
      i. Work on Strength, shore up weakness to avoid a fatal flaw

As I was exiting Deutsche, I had time to focus on myself. It was genuinely fun to explore. One of the beliefs that I have is that to be effective, we should work on our strengths and ensure that our weaknesses are managed sensibly.

If you are starting out or junior in your career, "The 360 Degree Leader: Your Influence from Anywhere in the Organization" and its complimentary workbook by John C. Maxwell are fantastic. [3]

I read "The Extraordinary Leader" by John H Zenger and Joseph Folkman [4] in the early 2000s. It became my Bible for managing people at work. It is based on solid research of 200,000 assessments of 20,000 managers.

My single takeaway was that we should build on our strengths so that they become extraordinary, identify our weaknesses, and work on them so that they are no longer roadblocks. Also, when some strengths are combined, then it is truly synergistic. I have used it for personal development as well as for mentoring and coaching people right through my career.

ii. Feedbacks are vital

In the mid-2000s, I was part of Thomson's Top Talent program, and I had the most amazing coaches, Jim Greenawalt and Sarah Dunn, [my boss], and I will always be grateful to them. They were able to inspire me and make me understand how my behaviors would be understood by others, including across cultures. A simple one was that our CEO was not sure if I had what it took to be a senior leader.

To address that, we broke down the issue. First, I went up to our CEO, thanked her for the feedback, and said I would be working on it. After analyzing the issue, I realized that one of the major causes was that I would land in NY utterly jet-lagged and not be sharp enough for the elevator pitches. I made sure that I started coming in a few days before the critical meetings. I would prepare myself for all the various interactions. Not only that, I would go back at periodic intervals for feedback to check if my behavior changes were noticeable.

This is very important irrespective of whether it was just

a *perception or* if it was *reality – either way, both need to be changed with different actions*. This kind of work is a life skill that one is building and is very useful not just professionally but also in our personal relationships.

A few of the dimensions that have always had an impact on my professional life are my physical state of well-being, mental/emotional states, and nurturing creativity. All these are self-exploratory journeys.

d. Physical Well-being
i. Do you have a fitness regime?

I have always enjoyed physical activities, even though I did not learn to build my endurance until much later in life. At school, I was always known as 'most enthusiastic' by my sports teachers. My swimming coach thought I had promise but totally lacked endurance. My hockey, basketball, and baseball coaches found me most uncoordinated. Hiking was fine as long as the slopes were not too steep! The part that has stayed with me is regular walking [*probably because it was a way to connect with my Dad*], yoga, and some form of martial arts, which today is TaiChi/ Qigong.

As a young person, I remember reading that Julius Caesar did not overindulge as he wanted to retain control. When Roman orgies were common, he wanted to keep his wits about him. I guess I never wanted to lose control; that meant that over the years, I built a strong understanding of food and supplements to stay healthy. Yet one thing I am still learning about is "Sleep."

Despite all this, I had fallen seriously ill, and the five years journey back to health left its mark. As I never wanted to go to the hospital for anything serious, again, I became very conscious of health requirements. I will take measures to remain healthy. Any minor issues were handled by various doctors in my family. At work, I will not show physical weakness, even if I have a minor flu. I will also actively build business continuity for my role.

ii. Compensating Practices

One of the consistent feedbacks that I received over the years is people commenting on how energetic I always appeared. In order to maintain a high energy level, I have actively cultivated a lot of techniques. I also knew my weaknesses, and I would proactively take steps to ensure that they were handled.

For example, during the crazy travel that I did for work, I would ensure that *I ate right, stayed hydrated, and exercised*. Sometimes, I would even *lie down for 15 minutes and do deep breathing* before the evening dinners.

My library is full of books on yoga, tai chi, karate, and Mayo Clinic's books on managing stress. During Covid, my cousins and I started learning *Kinesiology, a practice for self-care*. There are numerous tools and techniques within this field, and what appealed to me most was the protocol of recognizing an issue, reframing the problem into the outcome we want, identifying what is the emotional barrier that is coming our way, and then trying to address the issue. Example: There are tools to recognize what natural supplements are needed at a particular time. It also identified various Chinese energy meridian practices. This tool can also be used for other issues, such as why I procrastinate and avoid my personal paperwork. One can use Kinesiology for anything- health, relationships, or work. Irrespective of anything, it gives one a sense of control over one's well-being. Kinga Papp's website is a very good resource if you want to explore this field [5].

iii. Find your tools to support the life that you want.
- **Resources**

For me, physical health is all about feeling healthy in one's body – not weight. Exercise is about feeling happy in the body [*sukham asanam*, as my yoga teacher says]. We were in Scottsdale for a Senior Management meeting in January, and it was cold. I thought I would get a massage as my muscles were stiff. Unfortunately, I didn't get a slot for the massage, but I found the Yoga room empty and did an hour or so of stretches. It felt like a massage from the inside. I could move with ease. The spa also gave me some nice goodies!

Educate yourself on what the physical fitness regime is for you. It might be running, weights, sports, hiking,….. See what it makes you feel both emotionally and physically, not just how it makes you look.

There are a lot of resources out there, including your healthcare practitioner.

Don't worry about the ideal choice of book/podcasts; just keep exploring. If prior approval from your doctor is needed or trainer support is required, then please get it.

- **_Food and supplements_**

We all know when we feel 'good full' and when we feel sluggish and uncomfortable. My yardstick is from childhood when my grandma used to feed my cousins and me. We would feel full but full of energy to run around. The food was balanced yet with a bit of indulgence. That is my ideal meal. As we get older, we get more sophisticated in how we build this out.

When working an intense job, I was clear that I did not want fast food as it would mess with my health parameters, but more importantly, it would make me less effective at work. Talk to your doctor or nutritionist. Invest in learning about this – it is your health, and you need to be the driver. Today, there is a lot of good, easily accessible information, but go to a certified professional to ensure that you are on the right path.

- **_Sleep_**

It is only in recent years that I have understood the relationship between sleep and health. I come from a family that will actively compromise on sleep. I realize today that it has a serious impact on my stress management at an endocrine level, and I want to handle that effectively. Again, there are lots of free resources, yet it is important to get professional help. Start with using your Fitbit to monitor yourself.

The other day at a Board the team was talking about how they work late to meet targets on a monthly basis – as an Independent Director, my feedback was that I would be concerned with this style of working on an ongoing basis. It would affect their ability to scale up, but more importantly, they are jeopardizing their health!

Physical fitness is absolutely vital for one's success as a

professional. While I have done my share of all-nighters, I have learned to prioritize health over other things.

During Covid, it meant being at peak physical health – no food items that cause inflammation, exercise, supplements, and sleep, sleep, sleep!

- *Understand your hidden beliefs about health*

Recently, I came across a start-up that uses the gut biome to provide insights on what supplements can be used to improve your health for stress, sleep, and energy and for healthy aging and even Female reproductive health. It uses *Computational Biology / AI* to drive this learning. I am sure such start-ups will help us more in the future.

Yet we all have our baggage on how we manage health. A good colleague of mine remains a chain smoker; another is a fitness freak, and even though he always looks exhausted, a third never goes for check-ups. While I can't say I fully understand their beliefs, I think the first person's father died at a young age, even though he lived a good life. The second almost seems to be running away from the possibility of any health issues. While the third doesn't want to face anything that a check-up might reveal.

I marvel at the advances in medicine. Growing up with a Doctor for a dad, he inspired me to look at the discoveries and feel a sense of wonder. When I was in college, I discovered alternate holistic medicine, ayurveda, and homeopathy. It was a concerting to me that modern medicine was based on theories supported by empirical evidence. The fact that there could be other theories of healthcare was confusing.

Today, I no longer have the child-like faith in the medicine that I had earlier in life – yet there is an acceptance that I need to choose what is available to remain healthy.

We saw this play out during Covid, where despite misgivings about the vaccines, most of us got our vaccines. Like many others, I also have a 'white coat syndrome' as a residue of my illness. So, my compensating behavior is to do everything possible to remain healthy.

- ***Find your hidden beliefs and work with them.***

Your *physical health can impact your professional goals.* Being blessed with good physical health will enable you to become effective at what you do – an entrepreneur, senior leader, or an athlete. If you have weaknesses, e.g., I used to have migraines, then work on building compensating strategies.

My goal is to be healthy and manage my energy and stress.

iv. Emotional

In today's world, *we often use 'mental/emotional' health interchangeably.* Yet, while working on the LifeBook by John and Missy Butcher [can be found in Mindvalley.com], I realized that I can have emotional goals that can drive me towards top performance.

At work, we often compartmentalize and don't really bring emotions into the workplace. In recent years, senior leaders have been encouraged to exhibit their emotions to demonstrate that they are bringing their whole authentic selves to work. I remember a Board member doing this, and the rest of the team watching in shock and horror as everyone wanted to see strength but got someone who seemed to be falling apart. Read your audience!

My personality type clearly shows that while I can be warm, caring, and empathetic, I don't operate from indulging my emotions. I don't know how much nature vs. nurture is. Over the years, I have actively tried to recognize the emotions that drive me, understanding their impact on the physical body, my behaviors, and how they impact my interpersonal relationships.

I was talking to a new CEO, and he mentioned that he knows he has some 'off' days, and on those days, he hangs a sign that he is not available for ad hoc interactions. It was great to see this level of self-awareness and how he took action to manage it.

As a young person, I was very clear that I did not want to be emotional and have mood swings. Today, I recognize that emotions are nature's subconscious cues on how to deal with the world, and this is a vital tool to operate in the professional world as well. It is important to manage our emotions.

We all talk about our gut feeling, which we validate with data.

Depending on your *emotional status* and your aspiration, you may want to see how this *impacts your professional world.*

During the second wave of Covid, all the senior managers at our company were being trained to be Mental Health First Aid providers. My concern was that most of us had lost close loved ones [not singular but multiple], the trauma of others was re-opening past wounds for many. **We needed to take care of ourselves before we could help others,** just like they tell us in the airline briefings!

v. Mental Well-being

A few years back, our organization ran a psychometric tool called the Tetramap [6]. It was fairly simple, almost like a party game. It is actually a proven global tool for training and development and is used by businesses to transform team performance, energy, and motivation. Most of us would fall into 4 categories: Fire – ideas person; Earth – execution; Air – detail oriented; and Water – people. I remember struggling to work with one of my colleagues. It wasn't really a relationship issue but more about how we engaged at work. He was very detail-oriented and execution focused, while I was strongly ideas and execution-oriented. So, while we were aligned on execution, the way we arrived at it was completely different. Once one understands how the other works, one compensates for the other while we work as a team.

In recent years, there have been a number of people leveraging neuroscientific tools to drive peak performance. These 'bio-hacks', as they are informally called, are fun to try.

To be a top-notch professional, we may find ourselves dealing with various issues such as *brain fog and fatigue*, which are common outcomes of stress; it may be due to poor physical, emotional, and mental health. Don't be shy about reaching out for professional help, even while you practice self-care.

As I was leaving Deutsche, I was drained. I felt physically and mentally exhausted, and I knew I needed time out before doing something more serious.

So, I decided to explore, talk to people, and do mini-projects where I did not need to worry if I failed. It gave me time to step back before I started stepping forward. So, even if you have the most amazing professional goal that you want to take up, *check if you need to step back first to nourish your well-being.*

vi. Creative Pursuits

When we are in school, most of us are exposed to art, music, and performing arts. As we grow into our careers, we may retain creativity at work. Occasionally, some of us will keep our interests going by practicing art, music, and theater as a hobby, and some will at least regularly attend performances. Only those who are in the creative economy will fully practice the arts.

In the last few years, I picked up my drawing and painting. During Covid, I even tried to learn how to play drums. That 1 hour a week was almost meditative, though I suspect my teacher was relieved when I stopped. I could clearly see that I felt better and was more effective at work.

There is enough evidence to show that using both the creative and analytical sides of our brains is good for our mental health. There is an increase in the number of synapses between the right and left hemispheres of our brains with these activities.

We see many famous professionals who use these tools to be at their very best. Richard Feynman, a senior international professor used to complete paintings on many of his flights. He held exhibitions, and genuinely enjoyed the process. Feynman was known for playing his drums and his art. Think about what we are doing to nurture this for ourselves.

As you start a new phase in your professional journey, examine how you want to leverage creative pursuits to support this journey.

vii. Spiritual anchoring

Today, the conversation of spiritual grounding is difficult.

Everyone needs to find the inner anchor that supports them through whatever life throws at them.

Post Covid, we have seen a resurgence of faith. We have also seen a tectonic shift in technological evolution [a.k.a. AI], and this again needs people to find their *inner resilience.*

At work, we speak about being authentic and bringing your

complete self to work. During Covid, we were dealing with life-and-death situations on a daily basis. This is definitely not something that a corporate entity deals with. At a hospital, one may see active expressions of faith. In the army, there are chaplains and priests for the soldiers. Yet in our offices, this is not an option– today, we don't have a Christmas party; it's a year-end party.

In this environment, a young HR colleague who had just come off dealing with a grieving employee, finding hospital beds and medicines, told me how drained both mentally and physically he felt. He said his single biggest source of strength was his *toddler, who sparked hope and joy* for him. We all need to find that source – be it in family, nature, religion, or other practices.

It is important to see if your current and new professional journey is going to be supported by whatever inner practice you have or want to build. We all need our own ways to center or calm ourselves. Our professional space is fraught with competition. It is important to find the tools that help us.

I have not expanded on this as it is very personal, and hence, each person needs to find their own path. Eckhart Tolle, with his focus on "Now," has been an immense resource through the years.

viii. Social/Community aspirations and other parameters

I remember selling Tuberculosis stamps and cookies to raise funds in middle school. Over the years, there were many activities, but I never thought much of it, even while sponsoring programs in the office. There was always empathy and caring, but my personal philosophy is that I don't really have the wisdom to try to change people's lives. Just do what is possible at this moment.

Almost 25 years ago, a young woman in office wanted to run away from her family, who were trying to marry her off to some unsavory character. My usual belief is that I don't know what is right, so it might be best not to interfere. In this case, I got in touch with some social agencies and got her help, and I came to the realization that there are no perfect solutions or answers. We do the best we can at that point in time.

As I was leaving Thomson Reuters, Subrato Bagchi was

mentoring me, and he exposed me to the Ashoka Fellows and shared 10-12 CDs on Mohamad Yunus and Grameen Bank in Bangladesh [7] Social Sector was one of the options I was seriously considering exploring along with entrepreneurship. As the Corporate Social Responsibility law came into effect, I was fortunate to play a strong role within the company.

Around the same time, Harish Mehta advised me to be more engaged with the NASSCOM Foundation [8], and again, I was fortunate to be a Trustee on their Board for 6 years. I have also been engaged with the cancer prevention and poor patients' fund under Dr B.S. Srinath. Being a volunteer in the early days led me to be a Core Committee member at the Sri Shankara Cancer Foundation and Hospital [9].

As I left Deutsche, I became more active with Social Venture Partners svp.org and got involved in Fast Pitch, a program to support NGOs presenting their story for funding, and being a member of the Grants and Partnership committee.

As I experimented, I realized that I like size and scale impact, engaging with various NGOs in a time-bound, outcome-driven manner, and social impact commercial ventures. As a result of my various volunteering efforts, I was able to become involved with a couple of Non-Banking Financial companies with a priority on impact investment and with a Foundation driving livelihood and crafts as an Independent Director.

Explore what you want to do in the social sector. Test out different NGOs as a volunteer. Talk to people in that field. Try out different roles and see what suits you. Understand why this is important to you.

If there is something specific that calls out to you, go for it. Often, this is a vocation and could also be the professional step you take.

What are some of your beliefs in this area ...which ones become part of your professional endeavor, and which ones are perspectives that one may want to reframe for oneself.

ix. Digital competence

In today's world, being digitally and tech-competent is vital. Build this capability irrespective of what you do. You could be the next *digital media influencer or proficient in AI for your field or a cybersecurity expert?*

Do you want to impact the world, both digital and physical, through your actions? This might be worth exploring in conjunction with your need for recognition, fame, power, etc., and digging deeper into what the hidden drivers are. At the end, explore it, ask why it is important, and see how it fits in with your professional goals.

4. Resources

1. *Rich Brother Rich Sister by Robert Kiyosaki* and his sister Emi Kiyosaki. [10] The blurb in Amazon describes this book as "[this book]..will reaffirm your belief in the power of purpose, the importance of action, and the ability to overcome all obstacles in a quest for wealth, both financial and spiritual". For me, it was like yin and yang coming together.

Though it's changing, many Indians will have an ascetic shrinking from wealth as a goal. Hence, they are very happy to work for someone else but not chase a financial target through entrepreneurship. This book examines this topic from both a material and spiritual sense.

2. *The 4-Hour Workweek by Timothy Ferris [11]* came to me when I was in the middle of the Thomson Reuters merger. I was working 18 hours, and after 2 years, I felt drained and as felt though I was in a hole.

I had just got a fantastic role in strategy, even though it was a couple of levels below my role as MD, yet it was rejuvenating. I attended seminars on various topics, met new people, and learned about the changing world. It felt as though someone was paying me to attend school again! When I read this book, it was exhilarating: It gave me an insight into how I wanted to reconstruct my life.

At that time, as a friend of mine said, the Universe was giving me a gift of time when I missed a flight home and was stuck for a whole day. I used that time to decide on what I wanted to have, be, and do in the next 6 months and longer term. My version of what the worksheet in the book had for me was a dream life. It made me think, "Did I really want to buy X, or did I only want the experience of using it?" It also made me understand my competing priorities. Again, quoting from Amazon books, *"Being busy is a form of laziness."* At least 3 times per day at scheduled times, [Tim Ferris] he had to ask himself the following question: *Am I being productive or just active?".* Tim Ferris showed that *one could effortlessly be adventurous while being pragmatic, especially with one's finances.* That was when I joined Deutsche Bank!

3. *Happy Money* by Ken Honda [12] I came across this book shortly after leaving my job. For the first time in my entire adult life, I did not have a monthly income from a job. I was freaking. It did not matter that my accountant assured me that I had enough saved to live comfortably.

So even as my mind got these assurances, I was hyperventilating. A very simple technique that Ken Honda suggests is to say 'thank you' every time you receive, spend, or do anything with money. I found that this invokes a sense of gratitude every time one engages in financial activity, which is very empowering and made me realize that a lot of our issues around money are in our minds.

4. he last resource I want to share is *Christie Marie Sheldon*. I came across her YouTube video *"What are the 24 Abundance Blocks?"* [13] [14] A lot of the blocks are our fears and doubts that exist due to the different conditioning that we consciously or unconsciously have in the context of money.

5. When *Tim Ferris's 4-Hour Body [15]* came out, I was one of the first to buy it. It provides a lot of interesting insights, yet my strongest takeaway was about *optimizing my health to be a high performer* rather than preventing disease.

Yes, most of us want to get fitter only when there is a health scare. Do we really need that? Do we not enjoy waking up in the morning with energy, a clear mind working on all cylinders with a sense of well-being?

6. The 8 Colors of Fitness: Discover your Color-coded Fitness Personality and Create a Program You Will Never Quit by Suzanne Brue[12] [13]. Amazon describes the book as "a personality-based approach to a physically active lifestyle." This is based on the Myer-Briggs Type Indicator@ assessment, and based on this, 8 colors are identified, which provide one's preferences.

I am purple, and under MBTI, I am an ENTJ [Extroverted, Intuitive, Thinking, and Judgement]. This clearly showed me why I liked teachers who demonstrated what needed to be done, gently corrected me, but then left me to my own devices. It also gave me an insight into why I don't like gyms and competitions.

7. BKS Iyengar, TKV Desikachar, Lucy-Wyndham Read, Adriene Yoga, Rodney Yee, and, more recently, Shivananda Yoga have stayed with me. Breathwork, from the traditional Pranayama to Win Hoffman and even the simple Headspace apps, is a useful tool.

8. One of my favorites is John Assaraf's *"Innercise- The New Science to Unlock Your Brain's Hidden Power."* [16] [17]. It uses science-based mental and emotional techniques to strengthen your mindset. The Amazon description claims that the book will help you recognize and release your mental and emotional blocks, increase your self-confidence and self-worth, train your brain to focus, and eliminate your inner block.

What I found was that there are a number of interesting techniques that can help one become more effective, especially professionally.

9. Other resources include books by Wendy Suzuki[18], who talks about the neuroscientific approach to exercise, which improves one's brain function, and Huberman Lab posts Tim Bilyeu to improve productivity, impact, and effectiveness.

Exercise:
1. Identify your goals in each of these areas...........................
2. Recognize your beliefs underlying these goals......................
3. Understand why these goals are important.........................

4. *Which of these goals impact your professional goals*....................

5. *How will you include this dependency into your professional goals when deciding* ....

Conclusion:

Professionally, we do not operate in a vacuum, and hence, it is vital to consider all your goals, beliefs, and their importance relative to what you want to accomplish in your career.

Our navel-gazing does not stop here. We are also driven by our values, and it is important to check how this could impact our professional choices.

3
VALUES AND BELIEFS: THE "WHY" OF GOALS

Importance of Values in the Context of Your Professional Goals

25-30 years ago, people were fired from their jobs only if they had done something unethical. Today, reducing headcount is a tool used by organizations to improve performance.

- 25-to 30 years ago, recruiters often asked women if they would continue working when they got married. Today, it is not acceptable to ask this, even by law in many countries.

- Today, I am mentoring a startup for a community of women and LGBTQ+ to build their technical capability. Another startup is building tools to support people with visual disability.

This type of inclusion was definitely not part of the business world in the past. The above are just a few examples of how values change over time. As you start building your professional career, you need to be clear on what values are critical for you and what you will do in case you are not aligned with what is expected by the company or ecosystem. In fact, it is imperative that you examine the role that you want values and ethics to play in your life.

Why is this topic so dear to me? At Deutsche Bank, I have had the fiduciary responsibility in almost all my roles to take up the topic of Values, Beliefs, and behaviors. We were mandated by the regulators to drive this culture. Going further back in my career – I have been on boards from the beginning of my career and this is something I feel very strongly about. As someone said, 'Culture eats strategy'!

A friend, who is a regulator, shared when she read this book, "S, I wish I had known what you have written in this chapter, 10 years back!"

1. Historical context

Most national cultures have derived their values and beliefs from their religions. The modern world has tried to separate the state from religion, yet the values and beliefs still underpin our actions.

These values are common across all cultures and religions, yet the way they may manifest in practice has nuances that we need to consider.

This is called Moral Relativism. Ethics and religion are also closely related, yet in the business world, Ethics operate independently of religion, with secular philosophies providing alternate ways for decision-making. Values, beliefs, Ethics, and Principles all provide a framework to handle complex issues while maintaining social harmony, promoting empathy, and driving toward a more compassionate and cohesive society.

This is not a theoretical topic – international banks have a Culture as a board-level program often monitored by the regulators. There are specific metrics defined to track behaviors.

Having been part of these forums for a number of years, I am conscious of how important this is, especially in the financial sector.

2. Values, Ethics, Morals, Principles, Attitude:

The following section provides some basic perspectives on what the terms mean and an attempt to unpack how they may impact your professional arena.

i. Values

Values are society's shared beliefs about what is good or bad and how people should act. They are individual beliefs that motivate people to act one way or another. They serve as a guide for human behavior. People are predisposed to adopt the values that they are raised with. People also tend to believe that those values are "right" because they are the values of their culture.

Types of Values by which organizations operate include Integrity and ethics, Truth, Trust, Responsibility, Discipline, Commitment, teamwork/collaboration, Customer-centric, Performance-driven, and Innovation.

Think about your personal values and how they align with those of the organization you work with or are creating.

ii. Ethics

Ethics refers to both moral principles and the study of people's moral obligations in society. Ethical decision-making often involves weighing values against each other and choosing which values to elevate.

Conflicts can result when people have different values, leading to a clash of preferences and priorities. Ethics, therefore, attempts to provide a framework for functioning in society.

Today, business schools have Ethics as a basic subject in their curriculum.

iii. Morals

Morals are society's accepted principles of right conduct that enable people to live co-operatively. **Moral Relativism** asserts that moral standards are culturally defined and influenced by cultural, historical, and situational context; therefore, it may be impossible to determine what is truly right or wrong.

With multi-polar world and evolving geopolitics, if you are involved in any cross-border professional initiatives, it is important to be aware of these topics.

What might be acceptable in one country might be seen as a serious issue in another country.

For example, gifting policies are created to standardize the rules across geographies.

iv. Principles

These are fundamental rules or guidelines governing one's behavior to help govern ethical conduct, compared to values, which are qualities or standards of behavior. They are rules which provide the foundation for making ethical and sound judgments.

As someone who has been part of global teams, I have always felt it is vital to be sensitive about the principles in various countries. I have had to deal with a number of delicate situations arising out of these topics.

v. Attitudes

These tend to be opinions or stances that a person takes and are often driven by their personality.

Even when the values and beliefs are the same, the way they are handled can be seen by consequence management. Example: A murder has occurred. Leaving aside technicalities of first-degree murder/manslaughter, etc., what is generally black and white is that someone has been murdered. The challenges come based on what type of punishment is to be given. In some countries, a number of years in prison, sometimes running into 100s of years, is given; in another, life imprisonment is 15 years; while in others, Capital punishment is common, others rare, and in other countries, it is not applied.

These differences became very clear to me during the Thomson Reuters merger. Someone had misused an Amex card, and everyone agreed this was not right. It was the consequence management that proved to be fraught. One set of people was clear that the employee had to leave the company –i.e., had to be fired, with no reference. The most lenient approach that was considered was that he could resign and not be fired. Meanwhile, another set of people wanted to look at other options – as they felt that he was young, maybe his family took advantage of him, etc. This decision proved to be fraught as the 2 organizations were being merged, and this was one of the cultural/moral Relativism that needed to be resolved, not just for this case but for other cases in the future.

In that context, I liked what evolved in Deutsche, where a

committee would determine if something had gone amiss, and then a separate Disciplinary committee, constituted afresh for each case, would rule on the action to be taken based on facts and guidance.

3. Cultural Context of Values, Beliefs, Ethics – the WHY

A few years back, I attended a workshop on Richard Lewis's Culture framework. Richard D Lewis is a British Linguist, cross-cultural communications expert, and author. The Lewis Model is a framework for understanding cultural differences in communication. This model was introduced in his book from the late 1980s called, "When Cultures Collide: Leading Across Cultures." [1] It is based on the premise that cultural differences significantly impact how individuals from different backgrounds solve problems and work together.

The Lewis Model categorizes culture into 3 main types: Linear-Active, Multi-Active, and Reactive.

Linear-active refers to cultures that value time, planning, and structured communication. They prioritize efficiency and often follow a linear approach to tasks and conversation.

The Multi-Active cultures are ones where relationships and personal interactions are crucial. It's a culture that multi-tasks and places a high importance on emotional expression and social connections.

Reactive Cultures emphasize listening and observing before responding. They value harmony and indirect communication rather than confrontation. I'm not sure I like the nomenclatures, but in a very simplified way, the first group was the Western world; the second was the Latin and maybe the Middle East and Indian, and the last was the Asian cultures.

The workshop started with an advertisement for bread from one of the Nordic countries.

There was this young child of about 6 who was trying to get bread from the top shelf in the kitchen. In the meantime, the father sits at the table and lets the little fellow clammer onto a stool and then get the bread. After a lot of struggle, the child gets the bread, and the father has a faint smile on his face when he realizes this, as he continues to sit without moving.

In a Latin or Indian setting, not only would the parent get the bread but feed the kid and engage very differently.

The interpretation of the ad was that life is hard in Nordic countries, and it is important for the child to learn to become self-sufficient. This was an impactful eye-opener for me. I do not know if this is a correct interpretation, but as the trainers were from Europe, I assumed that it was accurate.

Though I am Indian, I realized that my professional behavior was more Linear Active. This meant my values of right/ wrong in a given context took precedence over my value of protecting relationships in the workplace. Yet, looking back, I realize that I have maintained the relationships just as much as I have held onto the 'right/ wrong' principles. Probably, as I had been working in multinational companies for years, my approach was a blend of both Linear and Multi-active.

When I joined Deutsche, one of my bosses was very curious about how I made my decisions; after I shared a few examples, he said, "Ah, I see you are a value-based decision-maker." A bank deals with a lot of sensitive matters: it is easy to define whether it is legally okay or not.

It is more difficult to check the issues of grey in terms of human behavior. So, decision-making as a group reduces individual bias.

A few years ago, I was interviewing for a role, and the MD from NY said, "I see that you are from Mount Carmel College, a good Catholic Institution." I love my school, yet this comment made me uncomfortable. Maybe he was just trying to break the ice before we started talking, but it did not seem appropriate as the emphasis was on the type of school vs. the quality of education, and I dropped out of that process. Sometimes, we would ignore this and still go ahead with the job.

In the late 1990s in the UK, I went through an assessment process, and I still remember that one of the feedbacks I got was to become more 'Anglo-Saxon' in my style of operating! To be fair, they were trying to ensure my success in the organization. Today, this would lead to an interesting conversation with HR!

So, if you are planning to work internationally, learn about how each culture operates and build sensitivity around the values.

4. Do Values Change with Time?

When I first joined a multinational organization, I told my bosses that I would not be okay with a hire-fire culture. I was assured that given that we wanted to build a new off-shore unit, that would not be an issue. As time passed, we would be driving efficiencies and would reduce the number of full-time employee requirements, but thanks to growth and attrition, we never needed to fire anyone.

Over time, my roles changed, and as the Global Head of Business Engineering, I had to drive efficiency and process change across the globe. Despite both attrition and growth, there were still some situations, especially globally, when there were direct job losses as a result of that work. I remember talking about this to my aunt, and she provided 2 perspectives – firstly, the entire outsourcing / off-shoring industry occurs with job losses and cost cuts. So, I could bemoan the karmic impact of the suffering that I was inflicting or think about the new jobs being created as the organization found ways to survive and thrive.

Secondly, business is not so binary, and I was asked to look for the highest good that the decision could lead to.

The same happened during the Thomson Reuters merger. Despite a potential 1800 role reduction, the team grew from 5,400 to 9000+, and we were able to redeploy the staff. I am still not sure that I would feel comfortable just laying off people without ensuring that they had a job somewhere. I guess that is why outplacement agencies are so valued.

Looking through the lens of time, today, Startups, even in India, are laying off people to meet business goals. I remember reading a statistic that most of us will be laid off at least 4 times in our corporate careers! This means we better build our resiliency muscle and have plan Bs for our careers.

As an employer, once you decide to lay off someone, act swiftly, be upfront, and do it with compassion, as it might be you on the other side on another day.

Here is where the personal decisions come into play. There was a situation where we had an amazing person on our team. Globally, he was as feted, and there were talks of him being elevated further. Unfortunately, he seemed to have rubbed off a lot of people while getting things done; some of these people made allegations of impropriety. Despite the lack of specific evidence, the global team deemed that this was not the noise we wanted. I pushed back to the extent that I could. Then, it was either to support the individual and try to save him or impact the complete team. We were at a delicate stage of growth, and after discussions with HR, we decided to support the decision. Emotionally, I felt an awful sense of guilt and betrayal, yet the team felt that there could have been no smoke without fire. Yet another international colleague of mine said, "You may want to think about the implications of 'guilt by association.'

I still remember getting totally chilled by this talk. What did Guilt by Association mean? - The company you keep speaks about your values.

Within a day or so after the above event, I was leaving for our Global Headquarters. As I was very disturbed internally, I decided to buy a return ticket with my personal money apart from writing my resignation letter to take with me.

At the HQ, I spoke to the leadership and shared the conversation about "Guilt by Association." I said that if they could not trust me and if our values were not aligned, then it might be better if I quit; I shared my letter and return ticket.

Fortunately, the leadership took a position of trust, and I stayed on with the organization for a long time. They had my back in a number of other situations.

On another note, I am still in touch with the person who had to leave the organization, as it is a case of innocent until proven guilty.

Most of the difficult situations throughout my career have been these kinds of dilemmas, and hence, the topic of values, beliefs, principles, and ethics forms such a strong element in my decision-making.

Just remember, sometimes values can change with time, both at a societal as well as an individual level. These can happen due to Cultural evolution – we have seen this change in the way business is now more inclusive of Diversity, Equity, and Inclusion.

Technological advancements are reshaping the world, and we will explore a bit more of this later in the chapter.

Education is a great leveler, and as we get exposed to new perspectives, we see more changes – as Thomas Friedman's book "The World is Flat" [2] clearly brought out. Economic changes also have a huge impact on human behavior – sometimes, it brings out the best, others the worst. Major events such as wars and natural disasters can lead to changes – any global traveler will share stories of border crossing and how things have changed.

For me, the underlying element is one of trust. Personal experience and generational shifts also play a major role. Yet, on another level, it is not as different as we thought; it is just the context.

As you are moving into your new career, job, etc., be pragmatic and see what types of situations you are likely to encounter and why that might pose a concern for you.

5. WHAT type of situations are you likely to encounter?
i. *Where you are going to work*

The company, country, type of function, etc. have nuances that you may want to consider in the light of your Values and Beliefs.

I remember a sales guy who we needed to let go after 8-9 months. He was fantastic and did a great job. Our revenues were growing strongly. Slowly, I started hearing murmurs from other sales guys and, finally, from the customers. In the previous organization from where he came, it was acceptable to engage with the Procurement leads in a way that we did not condone. We did not want to tarnish our reputation by resorting to those practices. We spoke to him. He promised to change his ways to be in line with the organization. We realized that the company would not be Trusted if we retained him. So, we did let him go.

In the 1990s, asking a lady about her plans to have a child, etc., was an accepted practice in India. In fact, even today, in many institutions, it still happens. As we built the off-shored center for Guardian Royal Exchange, we had to train our managers to ask neutral questions in line with various international laws.

Today, I find this still exists in pockets, and we may want to take a stand on what it implies if you are on the receiving end. How do you want to respond?

As the Diversity, Equity, and Inclusion movements have progressed, there have been a number of sensitivity programs to ensure we are genuinely supportive of different groups of people and becoming aware of our unconscious biases. The values of inclusion and ensuring equal opportunity need to ensure that no group is unduly distressed.

I have mentioned that in the mid-1990s, I had been seriously ill. I rarely shared this in professional circles except in vague terms, but every time I moved to a new role, I made sure that I disclosed it explicitly to my boss and HR. I operated in a world where the number of women managers was few, and I did not want to lose my opportunity to do a job because of a past illness.

Today, many cancers are not fatal. People discuss this disease openly. In fact, I recently learned that it is one of the disabilities defined by law. Yet in those days, it meant a potential job loss, no promotion, and being looked on with pity. So, it still remains a 'serious illness."

ii. *Type of Teams:*

For most of my career, I was the only woman in a team of men. In the last 10 years or so, in the international arena, I ticked off the checkboxes for woman, age, and Asian/Indian diversity. Yet, because I had got my MD position long before this kind of positive support, I was not seen as a 'diversity' candidate. This type of grouping can undermine one's confidence. I have seen a number of people questioning their competence because of this affirmative support. Make sure you build your inner self-confidence for what you are capable of doing.

A colleague and I were in Beijing, and we were talking about culture, both on a personal level as well as at a country level. We were talking about our responses to various situations which arose from our illness. It was diametrically different. I rarely talk about the specifics of the disease. I acknowledged it enough to go through the treatment and then pretended that everything else had happened in life as usual. My colleague, on the other hand, was very comfortable talking about all her experiences, including her feelings. She was British/ Australian, and I am Indian. Yet, we did not respond like people would expect from our national stereotypes. We shared this personal experience as a way to demonstrate how we can work in an international organization. It was one of the most liberating sessions as we took a truly raw and personal life-changing event and highlighted human responses and their implications.

For example, my colleague shared pictures of the day she lost her hair in the office with her office team around her, whereas in my case, most people did not see me during the transition, and most people did not realize that I was even unwell. I don't know whether I would have behaved differently today, even though I doubt whether there would be any overt discrimination. In fact, there would be more inclusion.

It was during this trip that I came across the concept of the Iron Woman in the Chinese business environment – someone who was strong-willed. They had to do a very delicate balancing act where they had to be successful internationally while being accepted by the local teams. This is probably true across many countries – a common gender experience. If you do encounter situations like this, think about its impact on yourself and choose what makes the most sense for you.

6. Character

The formation of one's character is yet another integral part of our life. It is comprised of your values, beliefs, and personalities, which come together to create a unique and individual identity. It is basically our own distinct narrative, a story that speaks about who we are and what we stand for. And character is an important element because that is who you are as a central person.

When we make a change and move ahead in our careers, the actions that we take today will have an impact on our lives maybe twenty-five years from now. So be conscious of your choices. I was talking to a young professional who wanted to grow in a highly technical and competitive field. The person also wanted to be known as a cool party person. When she realized that recruiters would be checking her social media, she decided to reshape what and how she shared her personal life. Unlike in the past, all our lives are an open book with social media. It is fantastic, yet it can be a challenge if your work and personal persona are very divergent.

Again, your values and principles will play a role in how you put yourself in the public domain.

7. Impact of Technology

The current trend of AI-driven job loss presents a difficult situation. Fourteen million people will be affected in the coming years, and while the company may require layoffs, you may want to see how this is going to affect you. A good friend who is a senior HR professional said that the constant round of layoffs was making him feel really burnt out and not happy with himself. He became an HR professional because he liked people, so he decided to pivot his career to become a life coach.

Strong self-awareness is needed to make life choices.

Long back, I was working in the share market and was constantly focused on the impact of external events on the portfolios that I was managing. One day, there was a serious disaster, and a whole business family died. My first response was to look at the share portfolio, not respond to the human tragedy. Obviously, as a portfolio manager, it was necessary to see the impact of the tragedy on the portfolio. Yet this experience left a deep impact, and I requested a role change as I did not want to put money ahead of human tragedies. It taught me that I need to listen to my inner self even if, on the surface, what I was doing was fine.

AI is also going to provide challenges of trustworthiness and personal values as it gets more integrated with our personal lives. AI is trained on existing data, which is often reflective of society's conscious and unconscious biases. For example, we may trust or distrust AI based on how it aligns with our values on data privacy or values of fairness and inclusivity, as there is significant cultural relativism.

AI Trustworthiness is contingent on factors such as Transparency of how the AI makes decisions, Reliability based on consistency of the AI responses, Fairness, and Ethics. Care needs to be taken that AI does not perpetuate or introduce biases that are not aligned with societal norms. Yet, this is not a simple binary.

Finally, societies with a high trust level with Digitalization may respond very differently from a culture where there is a trust deficit.

The reason why this could be important for you as you decide to go ahead with your professional goals is to assume you are an AI developer; are you conscious of your biases? If you are a researcher using AI, would you recognize biases in the information AI provides? Currently, most AI has been built by the Western world; if countries like India want an Indian lens for certain topics, say philosophy, art, literature, etc., then they need to build local LLMs, capturing the local cultural nuances. We also need to ensure that it plugs into the global AI construct so that the best of both worlds can be leveraged.

One of the use cases for AI is for medical drug discovery. Recently, I was with a startup working on gut-biome, and what was evident was that 98% of the current data comes from the Western world, and this company wants to build the data for India and other groups that are currently under-represented. There is also data to show that most drugs in the past were not tested fully on women. Yet, as women have 3 gonadal hormones versus only 1 endocrine hormone for men, there are now studies showing that there could be different implications of how a drug functions in these scenarios.

With more personalized drugs being created, this is a fantastic opportunity to ensure appropriate representation of race, gender, age, etc., which are there in various trials, thus ushering in a more holistic approach to health.

8. Do you speak up?

Most large institutions expect people to speak up, yet there are many situations where people are concerned about whether to speak up or not. Check what is important to you and when how you speak up.

I have seen people who have been in the Compliance function and who are responsible for calling out inappropriate behavior, yet if it affects them personally, they may not feel very comfortable calling it out. As head of various institutions and functions, I have always asked people to call out if things are not okay. I truly believed in the systems of the organization.

Yet there was a time when I shared an uncomfortable situation with HR, but I was not interested in going forward with a formal complaint. I thought I had a pragmatic view of what was likely to happen, including the stress I would feel going through the process of complaining. I am not sure what I would do today.

You are the best judge of what is right for you at that time. Even if you don't call out in public, please share your discomfort with the right authority so that they can take appropriate action.

9. Value-based Approach to Building a Business Portfolio

In the last 2 years, I have taken up various professional activities, including consulting.

As I left Deutsche Bank, a close friend advised me to:

- Not charge for my work if it's an NGO/ not-for-profit organization
- Ask for reasonable/deferred / non-cash payments from startups for your advice. (Free services are not always valued.)
- Charge a commercial rate for large 'for-profit' entities.

Long back, when I was at Guardian Royal Exchange, like many in the Indian IT industry, I was very free to share my advice with a European organization, including making a video for their global board, with my organization's approval. When they finally set up an organization in India, they felicitated me and gave me a gift. As per company policy, I shared it with my boss and asked for guidance on what to do with it. It was not something very large, so I was allowed to keep it. The company that recognized me said that if they had gone to a consultant, they would have had to pay a hefty amount.

For me, it was an opportunity to grow the industry and a really nice thing for the country. I think this collaborative effort was the hallmark of the Indian IT Industry, a value that you don't often see in other sectors.

I like taking up various initiatives, and I always try to find a larger meaning or purpose for what I am doing. I align this between myself, the organization, and the team. The day you're not able to find that larger purpose is the day you have to question whether you are just doing an activity / busy work or if it is something worthwhile.

Another event that could exemplify the importance of having your core values aligned with the system you are a part of is when you get involved in the healthcare industry. They have their own sales target, and apparently, their major mode of sales happens via doctors. We generally consider doctors as demigods, as they can save our lives, so when they function very commercially, it troubles us, especially if we think they have crossed some line that is often difficult to identify. As I was leaving my last job, I was talking to a Professor from Cambridge, and we got talking about the Agri-Defense-Banking- Pharma nexus and its implications on human values. We saw some of this play out during Covid.

It is important to ensure that your profession is aligned with your values, or else it will eat into you.

Exercise:
1. Write down your Core values, beliefs, and principles..................
2. If you have to make a decision about selecting your goals, how do you apply these values and beliefs to that decision? ....
3. You have already made your choice of your Professional Goal. Do you want to make any changes based on these values?................................

Most of us grow up with values, beliefs, and principles being shared through our parents, family, and school, and we may not know what it is until we are called upon to live it in our lives. On a personal level, most of us tend to be truthful and try to comply with laws.

Yet reports about India often speak about corruption levels. As a global manager, I had to do all that I could to ensure that the global organization never had a reason to question the India team. So today, when I speak to young people, I always ask them what they want their country to be known for. Are they doing all they can to build the nation that we want with our actions today?

Values are how people judge us. Shortly after I joined Deutsche, a number of regulatory investigations were being closed, and bank's behaviors were being called out. In most situations, we will find that the bulk of the people are law-abiding and reasonably sensible people. Yet a small percentage, if they are in leadership, they can create a culture which is not good. I got involved in the remediation and building of the risk culture, values, and beliefs. The number of meetings where I was involved in discussing the implications of ethics, integrity, and behaviors have clearly left their mark on me.

At a business forum, I was part of the national group that developed the code of ethics that companies could adopt. There were anti-corruption programs that we were keenly working on.

My dad was a Professor of Medicine in his later years. He used to always kick off his first class with a discussion on medical ethics.

I remember his first lectures, which he used to share with me. The result is I often push this dialogue with many of the startups that are scaling up.

The world is a complex place, often with nuances that are not always black or white.

At work, the first filter is - is it legal? If yes, then is it moral? If the answer is not black and white, then ensure that you have a group of diverse perspectives so that one can arrive at a more balanced response.

We had a situation where some young people had been caught behaving in a sexually explicit manner in the office during a night shift – even though it was consensual.

The people who reported to us were the security personnel who picked it up in the security camera. There was an intense discussion across the leadership team. The perspectives ranged from what it would look like if it were to appear in the newspaper – to potential reputational damage to the company.

At that time, during recruitment, we still had families checking out the office before the women joined [times have changed now]; we had to consider the impact on female recruitment if this went public. The security staff watched the leadership to see how we would deal with this matter.

At the leadership table, we had the full range of responses from: they are young; just tell them not to indulge in this type of behavior in office [they had already been told]; to folks who wanted them to be sacked. It was a delicate balance in terms of decision-making.

Offices are places that mirror society, and often, some of the societal issues get played out at the workplace.

Another situation was when we were selecting a manager for the night shift. The best person was a young woman. She was getting married, and the leadership felt that this would be an unfair pressure on her.

Yet her manager spoke up for the young woman and pushed the leadership to select her and leave the final decision to the young lady.

The young woman chose the job, and it turned out that her husband was also on the night shift! I truly felt proud of my team that day. They were open and willing to discuss and were happy to arrive at the answer post-introspection.

I remember another incident that happened a long time back when one of the young employees of our company, who was just married, came to the office in traditional attire wearing red bangles symbolic of a newly married woman. One of the managers found this inappropriate and was not comfortable with it.

Yet today, hopefully, the environment is more inclusive. Though there are subtle [or not-so-subtle] rules for dressing, it is fascinating to see what happens when we don't follow them.

I have often struggled with what the most appropriate attire to wear for each occasion is. While this is not a value, it is indicative of operating culture.

Conclusion:

We often don't think about the topic of Values, Beliefs, Principles, or expected Behaviors that will have an impact on our choice of careers. We want to do what drives our passion or goals, just like the old Buddhist value of "Right Livelihood" – we need to work out what that means for us. It is not just a means to earn a living; it's a lot more than that.

Some of my core personal and professional Values

Integrity, law-abiding, trust and honesty, mutual respect, personal accountability and responsibility, loyalty to the organization, compassion and gratitude, fairness, and transparency.

There are others, yet these are the ones that one works with most frequently.

My values and their impact on my profession

As I have shared a number of stories already, I will just share a few points. Before I join a network or organization or develop a professional relationship, I will try to align my values.

I take on a lot of things and try to ensure that I deliver [personal accountability], or I try to avoid taking on the responsibility. I take my mentoring very seriously – the mentee is a person sharing their dreams – understand where they are coming from.

An approach to reviewing goals vs value – what does that look like?

I wanted to contribute to something bigger than myself [part of my goal] – I checked out the people/ organization and the philosophical alignment and got it validated with people I know.

I recommend that you review your professional goals against your value system so that you feel truly aligned with your inner self.

In the next Section, we will reflect on Choosing the right option – based on your personal power, the impact of networks, and your ability to handle change and thrive in uncertainty and finally making your choice.

SECTION II

4
CHOICE TO DECISION-MAKING

For me, *choice is fundamental to a sense of freedom.* I have always been captivated by *Viktor E. Frankl's "Man's Search for Meaning"* [1] and the ability to choose even in dire circumstances. Hence, the entire first section, which is about finding our goals and values, is aligned with 'choice.' As we move forward, it becomes 'decisions' for action.

Choosing and decision-making are words that are used interchangeably, yet they originate from different roots. The word 'decision' originates from the Latin root "cut off," while the word "choice" originates from a root that means "to perceive" [2]. "Choice connects us to our desired intentions, values, and beliefs. Decisions are connected to places of behavior, performance, and consequences" [3]. The Forbes article of May 19, 2017, describes it as "The place of choice is the crossroads between feeling fulfilled and aligning with your own values. Only after you have identified the place of choice can you move on to the point of decision, which is where you finally consider all options and decide what to do.' [4]

This chapter is for the people who aspire to change – and emerge as the leaders and warriors of their lives.

Circumstances may be tough, but our responses and actions are what shape us and take us forward. This chapter provides insight into some of the theories of choice, decisions, and behaviors that drive us, including confrontation and procrastination.

1. Choice

Deutsche Bank was holding a women's conference in Singapore a few years back, and Sheena Iyengar of "The Art of Choosing" had been invited to speak. Her groundbreaking research on choice in 2000, known as the "jam experiment," was seminal. The research found that when confronted with a large number of choices, people would be attracted to explore them but unlikely to make their selections. When the sample set is smaller, then there is a greater probability of making a selection. This type of research is valuable in marketing and other areas where people need to select from multiple options. Such as policy-making, marketing, healthcare, etc.

This research made me understand why I tend to go into the first shop in a mall or rarely go beyond the first page during an online search. Too many choices paralyze me; this is called *Choice Overload*. When there are too many choices, after selection, we always feel that we might have missed out on some amazing opportunity – hence, there is *decreased satisfaction* from too many choices. The best example is at a restaurant with a menu that runs into 30-40 pages; one always feels that one has missed out on an amazing dish! Further, cultures can also play a role; for example, the US tends to be more individual-centric, whereas Japan is more of an interdependent society. This *cultural difference in choice perception is also important*.

Types of Choices need to be kept in mind when choosing: (i) Win-win, win-lose, lose-lose, (ii) *Dilemma* is a scenario where the multiple outcomes of the decision will be unpalatable. Yet, one needs to choose. Example between career and family. (iii) *Hobson's choice* - This is a type of dilemma where the options are between no choice and an unpalatable choice – for example, when selecting a political candidate. (iv) *Sophie's choice* is more of a moral choice with negative consequences that cannot be undone – in case of a disaster who gets aid? It is good to understand the types of choices as we are often faced with such situations.

As I left the corporate world, my choices were fairly simple: I wanted to explore areas of inclusive growth and change. I wanted the flexibility to explore my interests in innovation, art, or social impact initiatives. I wanted to distance myself from the past so as to not carry unnecessary baggage. So, most of my effort went into reducing the choices, ensuring that I was aligned with my goals, and reducing dilemmas.

Now let us explore Decisions.

2. Default Behaviors when confronted with choices or decisions

Let us start with an exercise to see what we understand of our default behaviors:

Exercise:

List out the type of situations when you
1. *Jump Head-on [instinctive]* ....
2. *Confront [conscious response]* ....
3. *Avoid decisions/actions* ....
4. *Procrastinate [Delay]* ....
5. *Deliberate decision-making* ....
6. *Do you know when & why you act differently [it will vary by situation]* ....
7. *Do you have a pattern that you want to change?* ....
8. *If yes, what are you aware of?* ....
9. *What action are you taking to change?* ....

It is important to understand what drives our behaviors as they manifest at the workplace

i. *Jumping Head-on and Confrontation*

Jumping head-on suggests a proactive, enthusiastic, energy-driven approach to tackling an opportunity or issue without hesitation, i.e., a strong action bias apart from high-risk tolerance coupled with a pinch of optimism.

Doctors, pilots, soldiers, firefighters, first responders to a disaster, and others who have to put in long hours of training will jump head-on into action when the situation arises.

They build unconscious competence to tackle any situation.

As people, we also jump into action with the best of intentions, but the outcomes may be sub-optimal. During Covid, we saw many examples of people reaching out to help – effort mattered.

ii. *Confrontation*

Confrontation has an implication that it is addressing a conflict, disagreement, or difficult situation in a direct, assertive, and open manner. It often implies taking immediate action with courage. It also indicates a personality that has a strong recognition of their strengths and needs for driving outcomes.

A factor to keep in mind when taking action without much reflection is that we either operate based on our default biases *[Confirmation bias]* past experience or just accept the new situation and act based on what is needed at that time. When I take on an issue head-on, I find that *I am able to refine ideas rapidly with greater confidence, and my ability to adapt, learn, and grow is higher.* I am not sure if I really call for data, evaluate it, look at comparisons, establish clarity, and act.

Confrontation is a response; for example, if someone is bullying you, you can proactively take it up or at least respond when confronted with it. This will happen throughout one's life, and we should build our responses to it. As my father started losing his ability to communicate, he found some of his caregivers being insensitive and laughing about his limitations. I remember him haltingly calling it. Even in that situation, he took back his power and dignity; maybe it was his years of training as a doctor and soldier that instilled this ability in him.

iii. *Avoidance*

Avoidance is actively steering clear of a task or situation. It can be a case of "don't poke the bear" or – *'Allow things to bake.'* We avoid situations when we fear failure, feel overwhelmed by the situation/relationships, and feel a strong emotional attachment. Often in business, there is the notion of the sunk-cost fallacy – i.e., we have already invested so much time, money, and effort, so we want to hang in.

When countries make laws, they don't generally jump into it. They test it out and watch others before moving ahead – we see this happening with laws around AI and copyright. Avoidance can thus be used consciously so that we don't rush and risk too much.

Avoidance as a tool: As we were scaling up the company, we had a group of recruits who were aggressive, almost eco-warriors. We decided 'not to poke the bear' but to see how the situation evolved.

Within a short period, things settled down when they realized that they could practice, but they also needed to carry people along and not push matters.

Avoidance as an approach can also be leveraged in personal situations. A few years ago, while working for Thomson Reuters, I was at a public industry forum. I was completely exhausted after a long stint of travel with its attendant jetlag. A mentor of mine, who was also there, said, "S, you look exhausted." So, I shared my travel schedule and said, "Yeah, I'm really tired." He said, "S, you are here to inspire other people, put on your game face! "I realized the seriousness of what he said because what is the message you're sending across to others? *Avoidance of such a situation may be the best; otherwise, learn a few tricks to manage it.*

'*Allow things to bake*' – during a change process, we start with creating an awareness of why the change is important. If the environment is not ready, I have found change programs will not take off. For example, when pushing for paternity leave in the late 90s, even after passing the policy, very few people used it. Today, it is culturally very acceptable.

iv. *Procrastination*

Procrastination is delaying or not completing an action due to one's inertia. I came across the phrase, *"Procrastination is a way of shutting down the future." [by someone Unknown].*

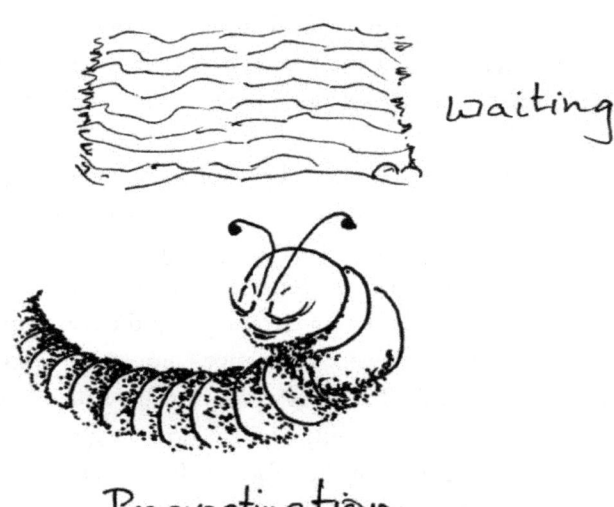

I was once mentoring a female founder. She had been amazingly successful in her design career, and she wanted to pivot to designing products so that she would not always be in a sales development mode. It was great that she had this self-awareness. She kept delaying, as she did not want to explain to her family that she was going to step away from a successful career to start something new.

Her first strategy was avoidance and to procrastinate having the conversation so as to not deal with emotional fall-out. She kept her dream until she applied for an entrepreneurial program. Once she got accepted into the program, she could no longer avoid the conversation with her family. To her surprise, she found that they were extremely supportive.

One of the common issues that many founders have is their aversion to documenting their business plans, cash flows, etc It is all in their heads. This interesting blog calls out what a founder needs to do. See if you resonate with *10 Common Small Business Mistakes to Avoid,* [5]

Always pick up the most uncomfortable issue first and deal with it. Often, it is a people issue!

One exercise that helped me *deal with procrastination* was *defining* my professional *goals and marking them on a calendar.* Look at your calendar and see where you have really spent your time. *If your goals and your activities don't match, then align them.*

We often give excuses that we don't have time or we are perfectionists, yet by delaying, the issue festers and gets bigger. As psychologists would say, this causes cognitive dissonance, leading to internal conflict, which leads to rushed and impulsive actions.

Some simple methods to control your Procrastination Behaviors:

- *Goal setting*
- *Time management*
- *Task visualization*
- *Accountability*
- *Time tracking*
- *Self-discipline techniques*
- *Distraction management*
- *Positive re-enforcement*
- *Mindset shifts*

The best techniques I found were from kinesiology, which enabled me to recognize the emotions that were the true barriers to my procrastination. Example: It has been a few years since my father passed, and I have not cleared his personal effects. At first, I felt that it was too soon to do so. Now, my excuse is that my mother may not be comfortable with my giving away my dad's stuff. Yet I think *it's my own inability to let go of various emotions that is the true barrier to action.*

Find your barriers to Action!

v. **Deliberate Decision-making**

According to research, we take 70-80 decisions a day – most on auto-pilot. Yet we are being asked to deliberately change lifestyles for better health, change our habits to improve productivity or learn new things – all of them require active decision-making. Given this, we need to understand how we can be more effective in making decisions.

I made a couple of very deliberate decisions during this period of transition: consciously letting go of my corporate career, making decisions around joining boards, and finding new initiatives and networks. One of the most deliberate decisions was to write this book.

When Raam got in touch with me, I said yes to writing the book as it was not something I had done before. I thought it would be a great learning experience.

The process was good – from trying to understand why I wanted to write to pick the target audience and the topic, then drawing up the outline, and then writing. Initially, I thought it would be easy - but my corporate training is to communicate with as few slides as possible; for a book, you think in 1000s of words per chapter! It was only in the last few months that I truly committed to the book.

Deciding is not enough; commitment is essential.

Let me share a story from a few years back. The organization was on the cusp of growth. We were informed that the global board would be visiting us in two weeks for a couple of days. If we got the global buy-in, then we would grow from ~300 to ~3000 people within a couple of years. At that time, I was the country head, but I did not know whether I would have the chance to lead this growth.

We, the team, while inexperienced, decided that we needed to 'Wow' the 8-10 board members. To do that, we did our research on them and then created over 40 POCs [proof of concepts] and aligned the right communicators. Personally, I was determined that the team had to win, irrespective of my personal future. The week was intense, and we won them over. At the end of the visit, I got a fist bump from the Chairman, and the Group HR told me that meant I had the job to lead the change! *Carpe diem! [We seized the day!]*, i.e., we confronted and won the opportunity. By not focusing on individual effort, I took the pressure off myself. We often see this type of behavior in sports – committing to the larger goal and winning both individually and collectively.

3. Decision-making Process

"The decision-making process is a multifaceted undertaking and requires multiple perspectives to handle all its nuances and complexity" from *Information Fusion and Analytics for Big Data and IoT*.

It is not something that happens automatically or overnight; rather, it is something that requires your attention and sensibility. The way you make a decision can have a huge impact on whether or not it works for you. All life's decisions come with consequences. It is not possible to fully understand what the consequences can be – just that there are no free lunches. Use the tools you have and then go into action.

i. *Establish clear Objectives or Goals*

Example: When I became head of Business Engineering, my goal was to reduce headcounts and costs and improve controls to manage risks. The board approved very specific, measurable targets.

If it is not specific, then it is a wish statement – for example, "I want to be involved with policy." – in what way? How will you contribute? Where and when will you engage?

ii. *Information Gathering*

Before making a decision, it's essential to gather data in order to understand the situation and analyze the options ahead. In the above situation, I worked with McKinsey to understand the processes and see where we could implement 'straight-through-processes' to make the back-office operations effective. For most decisions, we need 40-80% data to make sensible choices. Too much information will make you lose sight of the big picture; too little data will make the decision sub-optimal.

iii. *Alternatives, Criteria, and Evaluation of Alternatives*

Identify alternatives and then evaluate the options before final selection.

As part of the business process engineering efforts, we identified many alternate solutions. For example, consolidate teams to create large horizontal functions, develop a culture of constant improvement, and leverage technology for big and small changes. We then selected the ones that best suited us to delivery.

iv. *Culture-driven decision-making*

At Thomson Reuters, we were looking at building a wealth management product for the Indian market. One of the biggest takeaways for the global team was the way Indians made their wealth management decisions after consulting with their families, friends, and trusted advisors. Meanwhile, their Western counterparts tended to keep it private with only their wealth manager.

While building products, this was an essential factor to be included.

For the Business Engineering example – for the India teams, it was always good to go for constant process improvements or create consolidated horizontal teams to take advantage of scale. Internationally, it made more sense to build controls and system changes, given their subject matter expertise.

v. *Collaboration*

A team-building exercise between ops and tech demonstrated very different styles of collaboration. The ops team gave their input to the leader as part of the analysis and feedback and then allowed the leader to set the pace. The Tech team was more 'open-source' and democratic in their approach. Both are very effective, but their collaboration styles are different.

vi. Implementation

A few years back, I came across the phrase *"Thought to Action,"* which is the opposite of *"Blank canvas syndrome"* [which is a state of paralysis one faces when starting a new project – like a painting!].

Action needs to be initiated, even if it is baby steps –

Kaizen, constant improvement, shows visible results that the teams can own. Taking action will get you out of a slump – that is why people say clearing helps change one's energy.

There are quick and visible changes.

There is a lot of neuroscientific research to support the value of completing action.

Obviously, for larger programs, one needs to plan and think through, but start with some action – get a group together, set the agenda, or if you are pivoting your career, start with updating your LinkedIn or your CV. Reach out to a head hunter or a mentor to discuss your professional goals.

vii. Success criteria

Define the success you want to achieve. It can just be the activity for the day, or it may be a major deliverable. I find spring cleaning cathartic and makes me open to new things or working on a transformational activity [whatever that means for you]. It may be small things or truly massive. Keep the energy moving forward.

Imagine you have to do something that you really don't like; for example, you have to clear up your grandparents or parents' papers after they have passed away. Apart from being dusty and time-consuming, it is emotionally traumatic and tiring. While you can postpone it for a while, you don't have the option of skipping it. How do you deal with it? One step at a time! Chunk it up and tackle it at scheduled times – at one shot, over a couple of weekends, or daily for a few hours until it is completed. Sometimes, it may still not work, but don't worry; it's okay. Don't beat yourself up. Try something else. Maybe cleaning right now is not what you need. Maybe you need to find a bunch of people who are beautifying the city or painting all the dirty walls. Join them and clean up the garbage, or go for a run with that group.

Honestly, what you do doesn't really matter. It's a way of shifting gears and moving away from what feels like a setback or a rut.

If you're feeling low because you are not physically at your best, then **give yourself permission to rest.** Sometimes you just don't have the skills – practice until you get it right. It's okay to not be perfect. Especially in today's world, we don't give ourselves enough permission to just BE. We don't just sit and laugh. If it is something more serious, do not hesitate to see a doctor or counselor.

Try to identify the action plans that you are making to shift to the next phase of your career. Did you consciously choose what you want to do, or are you just being dragged along by life? This will ensure that you don't need to blame external circumstances or people for your choices.

Especially when life seems totally out of control, **pick a few activities that you can control.** During periods of intense change, I have often turned to focused martial arts, even if it was just twice a week. At another time, I used to bake biscuits or bread as my career was going through a lot of uncertainty. I even explored clay modeling. These activities gave me a sense of control. It was my work that gave me a sense of control when I was not well.

I am truly grateful that I have had enough people who have helped me out over the years! All these activities gave me a sense of control when life felt completely out of control! When things are uncertain in one sphere of your life, try something that you can control - it could be clearing out old things in the house, walking, golf, cooking, charity work, mentoring, or anything that shifts your attention to something concrete and makes you see results reasonably quickly. Try a before and after picture. Things may not go away, but it gives perspective.

viii. *At the Point of Decision*

We have the data and the options, yet what state of mind are you in when making an important decision?

Energy levels in action; reviews and feedback from stakeholders, including yourself; risk assessment, team dynamics; the role of intuition and experience;

time constraints and self-awareness of our behaviors. All of these factors impact our decision process.

I usually feel that action gives me more energy even when the task is tiring. Check out what your professional goal is doing – is it energizing you or draining you? If it is draining, is it temporary or ongoing? If it is ongoing, then you should consider changing the goal. That is what I felt when I continued with only risk, regulatory, and governance work – it became draining. I operate best when I am involved in growth and change activities when I have enough downtime to just rest, engage in intellectually stimulating discussions, and do art/exercise. It is the balance between being relaxed and pushing myself.

Do you have the energy to make the right decision? What state are you in when making an important decision?

Over the years, I know that I am very comfortable with an *uncertain environment*. Yet, I did not jump into a completely unplanned professional life until I had some degree of financial security. I would have no qualms about taking on professional challenges even if I knew nothing about that field, as I always felt that I could learn. I realized that there were a lot of people like me when I attended a closed-door event where Mohnish Pabrai, founder and managing partner of Pabrai Investment Funds, managing over $ 1 billion assets, was talking about his book "Dhandho Investor," [6] and I realized that it described my way of working. I am comfortable with uncertainty, and I have *safety nets for risk management*.

During my Thomson Reuters merger days, I had my team build a fairly sophisticated *Stakeholder map* – traditionally, it means a visual representation of individuals or groups with a vested interest in a project, product, or idea. One identifies the individuals/groups, scores their level of influence and engagement, and then builds a plan for addressing areas for improvement.

We built the map in Excel for over 500 stakeholders and then built plans of action. My biggest learning was that just because people are engaged, it does not mean that they will help with the outcomes.

Today, I use a lightweight version of this approach in *every interaction and try to create allies.*

Intuition and Experience: Gut/ Lizard Brain vs. Conscious Choice – while analytic tools are crucial, seasoned decision-makers often rely on their gut feelings, intuition, and past experience. Today's neurosciences are providing a lot of insight into how this works: being visual, creating contrasts, using beginning and end, using emotions, keeping it simple, make it specific and personal.

The decision-making process engages multiple brain regions, including the pre-frontal cortex [for weighing pros and cons] and the amygdala [emotional response]. It is believed that intuition may bypass the slower and more deliberate process, as the book *Blink: The Power of Thinking Without Thinking"* by Malcolm Gladwell shows. [7]

Emotional memory and intuition are incredibly powerful, yet they can be clouded by cognitive bias. It is important to recognize the lens of emotion from which we act. It is both a strength as well as a weakness. The other day, I was talking to an aunt of mine about one of my childhood adventures – hiding in the school bus instead of getting off at my drop-off point, as I wanted to know what happened after I normally got dropped. For me, it was a big adventure full of fun; for her, as an adult, she had seen this as a dangerous escapade.

Ethical consideration: We covered this topic extensively earlier, but let me share a story. I remember attending a senior management session of the Thomson Corporation in Scottsdale, and Carly Fiorina came in to speak. Her board was getting her to step down while she was on her way to speak at the World Economic Forum. I remember her speaking about her internal compass and how that held her even when the whole world outside was operating differently. Many at the senior management conference were very taken with this, yet there were skeptics who thought this was a façade. For me, it felt real, as my internal compass is very important to me.

People pleaser: Why do I include this in decision-making? If you are temperamentally a people pleaser, you are likely to take this into consideration – are you making the decision to please someone or because it is the right thing to do?

When I was part of the Thomson Corporation's top talent program, one of the assessment tools was to see how much of a people pleaser one was. Certain cultures and a lot of sales folks tend to be people pleasers

I had a 40% score, which was the highest for my small team of 6-8 people. Yet among Indians, I have a low score as I don't have a high need for pleasing. This awareness can be of value when one is working to shape one's career. I realized that my temperament certainly gave me a fair amount of freedom!

This is not an exhaustive list, but what this shows is that even when dealing with facts for making a decision, there are a number of implicit and explicit factors that play a role.

4. Post Decision

Communicate the decision to critical stakeholders and ensure you have a Contingency plan.

Having gone through multiple mergers, one of the corporate lessons is the need to communicate the decision to the stakeholders along with our rationale and expected outcomes. Often, decisions would need to be made in sync with your partner – a co-dependent decision or taking into consideration the feelings of another person [e.g., child, parent, team]. The time invested in communication is worth it.

On a personal level, you need to carry your key relationships along. As a parent, if you need to move for your job, you may need to ensure that your child has enough support for this transition.

Communication is key.

Despite all the planning, the decisions may not always work out, and we will need to go back to the drawing board to carve out another path. *Today, I am more relaxed about my decisions, and that is maybe because I am not afraid of failure.*

i. Execute – Action

Action: I like to take a bit of time before acting. Plan the action, break it down, prioritize it, and sequence it. Schedule it for the day, week, month, 6 months, 12 months.

Focus on immediate actions, even if the longer-term steps are yet to be worked out. Establish clear guiding principles and guardrails for the long-term deliverables to be agile and nimble to adjust to changing conditions. Life is unpredictable.

What do your activities make you feel? At one time, I had a number of initiatives that I was working through; at the end of each day, I would recall the emotions that each of the actions made me feel - positive, stressed, or bored. Feelings are a great barometer of how your inner compass is assessing your actions. Test it out. It's a good way to weed out the non-essentials. Sometimes, the work that makes you feel low may be financially most rewarding or supporting your family's needs. You need to consciously choose what is more important to you and then figure out how to motivate yourself in the work you are doing.

Let us look at post-decision-making.

Celebrate! Celebrate! Celebrate with each step!

Exercise:

1. Identify 3-10 things that will reinforce your feelings of accomplishment.

2. Review the answers that you may have written down for the P-Grow questions. Which ones energize you ……………………………..

I remember an interesting exercise where I was asked, **"*How do you celebrate your successes?*"** I realized that I don't actively celebrate my success. I don't let myself dwell in the feeling of joy for having accomplished the set of activities or deliverables. One of the other exercises was that I was asked to look at my to-do list at the end of the day and consciously think of ways to celebrate what I have completed.

How to celebrate: It could be to hug someone, even your dog! Share the joy with a loved one. Get a piece of chocolate, dance, watch a movie, or just do something that the brain associates with celebration and joy! Get creative about it, as it will associate effort completion with positivity. There is a lot of neuroscience literature that shares a number of hacks to improve productivity through these types of tools. Explore them – that in itself is fun!

What is your celebration ritual?
....

5. **Tools and Techniques for Decision-making**
    i. **SWOT Analysis-** Evaluate the Strengths, Weaknesses, Opportunities, and Threats of the situation. I often recommend this to any team that is resetting and moving ahead. I also used this personally to gauge where I would be most effective as I pivoted my career.
    ii. **Decision matrix –** Establishes some criteria to prioritize and compare the list of options. This is simple – for example, I want to know if a certain activity will create abundance, and if I need to compare it with another, then I can set this up fairly quickly. It helped me to say no to a few of the boards.
    iii. **Cost-benefit analysis –** Used in business, it is also effective for assessing our professional choices. It is important to know if you are getting the right return professionally. It can be for a job or for a business venture. I have said no to some consulting assignments. I have also found that sometimes, it is better not to charge for a service than to undercharge.
    iv. **Risk Assessment –** evaluates potential risks associated with decisions, as well as probability and impact. When joining boards, I always check out their financials, the various reports, what people on the street say about them, and whether their governance and compliance culture is aligned with mine.
    v. **Brainstorming –** Shortly after leaving Deutsche, when I went to meet one of the leaders in innovation in Delhi, I brainstormed a bunch of ideas to share with him. This is usually done in a group where all ideas are captured and then filtered and prioritized. When I shared the ideas with him and his team, it became a true brainstorming session. It is a good way to just see how one can solve a problem or solve an opportunity.

vi. **Mind-mapping–** I have used mind-mapping during my Business Engineering days. It's a great visual tool to structure the information, including their relationships, and help see the patterns and generate new perspectives. There are a number of apps that make it easy to use and help with great presentation, though I have not used it much since those days.

vii. **Six Thinking Hats of Edward de Bono-** I have used this tool at a certain point in my career. As we were scaling up the company, we wanted as many perspectives as possible so that we could be ready to manage the growth. We had a facilitator who leveraged the group to wear different hats to look at the issue and solve the problem. It helps me to break out of my *normal way of thinking*. The 6 colored hats are: White for objective thinking – facts and logic. Red for intuitive thinking and focuses on emotion and instinct. Black is for cautiousness to predict negative outcomes. Yellow is optimistic, looking for positive outcomes. Blue focuses on process and control for the next steps and action plans. Green is for solutions, alternatives, and new ideas. It is not commonly used these days, but I still like it for forcing me to look at issues with multiple lenses. Scenario Planning Involves envisioning different future scenarios [both optimistic and pessimistic] and assessing the feasibility and implications of decisions in each scenario. I did a number of these. What if I do not get any revenue-earning opportunities once I leave Deutsche? How do I have an independent director role in a company with dodgy practices? How do I make more time for interesting initiatives?

viii. **Darshanas –** I came across this approach after leaving Deutsche, and I have not used it except experimentally, but it is interesting. This is based on ancient Indian Philosophy, where there are distinct ways in which each philosophical system looks at things. As I was leaving my corporate career,

I met Shipla Dattar of Swayam, an Ayurvedic Psychometric testing organization. The founder was very kind to share the thinking behind the 6 approaches: Samkhya, Yoga, Nyaya, Vaisheshika, Mimansa, and Vedanta, and the atheist approaches are Charvaka, Jain, and Buddhist. It was fascinating. Yet, I don't feel I understand it enough to use it in practice.

There are a number of other tools which I have used over the years. If you are interested in this field, go ahead and explore. There is plenty of material in the public domain.

Conclusion:

As we go through life, we are constantly choosing, deciding, and committing to certain actions to achieve our goals. Sometimes, these go smoothly, yet at other times, things don't fall into place, and we need to plod on until one can ***finally be in the flow! Everything eventually happens at the right time.***

When I started exploring what to do next, it was fun, yet by the end of the first year, I was getting stressed – I had a lot of interesting meetings, but they didn't seem to be coming together. I realized I had to commit to certain actions and make some decisions. Once I did that, it got a little smoother.

This chapter introduced you to some of your default behaviors for action, tools for decision-making, the challenges of choice, and procrastination. With more awareness, we have a greater ability to operate consciously.

In the next chapter, we will explore the human dimensions of emotions and their impact in the context of networking.

5
NETWORKS:
THE HIDDEN INFLUENCE

Growing up in a defense family meant that one moved to a new school every few years – 6 schools were on par for many army brats! As soon as one joined a new school, one looked for kids with similar interests and aspirations. When one was younger, it was to look for kids who played the same games or painted or whatever seemed to draw them together. By middle school, the army brats would bond together to talk about their nomadic life in addition to common interests. As they got older, they joined the groups who were going after similar professional or future studies in addition to the extra-curricular activities.

Over the years, I developed this ability to join a new group and quickly assimilate. Despite this ability, I was a shy kid who was happy to be on my own. Guess that is why, in my P16 personality score, I was seen as an extrovert who did not need external validation.

As I was finishing school, I hung out with the kids who wanted to go into medicine. *This community had a purpose-driven engagement in all its interactions, and it was very energizing.* When I decided not to go into medicine and joined the undergraduate science program, I did not find the same drive in my college mates. The driven people had gone to medicine/engineering schools.

Looking around, I found the students in the arts courses to be the most vibrant ones. So, I switched and took up arts. Yet most of them were not clear about their professional goals even though they were very smart, with some going abroad for future studies and few opting for administrative services. Today, many of these women are truly successful in their chosen careers.

The reason for sharing these experiences is to show how strongly *we gravitate toward our tribe and our networks, which can support and influence our decisions.*

As I evolved in my career, NASSCOM [1] became one of my go-to networks – [*this is the business forum for all the Technology and Technology assisted enterprises in India*]. I would diligently attend the major leadership events and go to every activity planned there. Over the years, I had a network of truly amazing people, some I engage with often, some very rarely.

During my Thomson Reuters merger days, my boss once said

that I probably knew someone even on a remote island!

Getting into networks was something I knew how to do, but *leveraging the network actively was not something I understood* very much. I had this epiphany when I attended a reception for the US Sec of State as a NASSCOM Executive Committee member. A number of my ex-colleagues were sharing all the challenges that we had with visas, travel, etc., to the US. I was slowly feeling more and more uncomfortable. It did not seem polite to be pushing so hard with personal agendas. It was only later, with some reflection, that I understood the role of a business forum. *This network represented the business community, and as members, it was our role to call out the issues that needed to be addressed.*

Today, if I am going as a representative of a group, I have no qualms pushing the agenda of the collective. This is very important – whether it is for the DEI community, the startup forums, or a housing society. *In a network, we are not there as individuals, but as members of the community, and hence, as the voice of the group, it is important to speak up.*

In fact, in another instance at NASSCOM, we had to go and speak to the central minister on the topic of women's safety, and I recall speaking up and pushing back on certain expectations. That is the role one plays as part of a network. *It's where personal and collective agendas align.*

1. Importance of Social Capital in a Network

I have never explored the concept of ***social capital***, yet almost all societies around the world have had this as one of the tenets of an operating society. Most of us have rebelled or conformed based on our temperament to what our parents and teachers have expected of us.

In simple terms, Social Capital is the set of common values and resources that allow individuals to work together in a group to achieve a common purpose.

It fosters trust among its members, enables the group to work harmoniously, and ensures that the members of the group get value so that they continue to engage with the community.

In business, *social capital is vital for building trust, reciprocity, and relationships, which are necessary to facilitate opportunities and growth.* For example, a former boss could tap you for a new role; a business acquaintance could reach out to offer opportunities. This is dependent on your behavior and the perception that you have created.

I have usually met my commitments. Yet once I dropped the ball, it left a lasting consequence, and I have not yet recovered fully from that relationship. I had made a commitment to speak at an event. At the same time, at work, we had a board member who was visiting. My meeting with the Board member got moved, and I had to drop out of the speaking assignment at the last minute. The organizer has remained a good friend, but I have not been invited back to speak, though we still collaborate. *It only takes one situation where you drop the ball for social equity to be eroded.*

In life, this is bound to happen, and it is therefore important to continue to build equity so that when one drops the ball, the erosion is not final.

2. Importance of Networks
i. Networks support Growth and Change

Growing up, many of us are told that *the peer group we hang out with matters.* Today, management gurus say the same thing. Be with the kind of people you want to become - that will help you in many ways. Therefore, *Networks,* both *social and professional, hold significant importance in various aspects of life.*

As I was moving out of my corporate career, I reached out to my network, and many of them spoke about getting involved with The Indus Entrepreneurs [2], a global organization that supports startups. TiE's purpose is to help startups with learning, mentoring, and network connections, providing insights at the industry levels and helping with access to resources from accelerators to funding and often senior charter members. Those who have worked with the startups will act as champions and sponsors. As a Charter Member, I truly enjoy supporting the startup community. Now, if you are a startup, a community such as TiE, NASSCOM, or any other business community that supports your aspiration is a great place to engage.

ii. Networks support Career Advancement

Networks, therefore, play a critical role in **Career Advancement** both for entrepreneurs and those wanting to find a job. For entrepreneurs, networks are vital for finding investors, partners, and customers. Even as one scales up, a strong business network can lead to growth opportunities. Every time I mentor a startup, I think of opportunities where they can build partnerships, suppliers, or funding.

iii. Networks enable Knowledge and Information Exchange

Knowledge and Information sharing is critical for professionals. *I enjoy those networks where I can share information.* Being a member of multiple networks, *I tend to cross-pollinate information and ideas, which can spark discussions and perspectives.* As someone who got co-opted into being an Intellectual Property champion, I was able to share my passion with the startup community. Hopefully, the tribe of IP creators will grow.

There are people who go deeper and become subject matter experts. It is *worth investing in building the network in your areas of interest and expertise.* Someone I know who is extremely introverted is able to contribute immensely to the community due to her interest in the specialized field. These networks, therefore, help one exchange info and knowledge and develop new skills, and with today's fast-changing world, they become a lifeblood for information exchange for the professional. *We can get information from various feeds, but it is the personal perspectives provided by members of the network that lift your understanding to a deeper level.* Today, as part of the think tank with many professors and fellows there, I feel the need to read and write papers, although it was not what happened in my corporate career.

iv. Networks provide Emotional Support

As I was leaving the corporate world, I had my family and friends, yet the professional network that I had built over the years provided amazing ***emotional support.*** They *shared* their *experiences* of how they transformed themselves. Others *connected me to people* who, in turn, helped me *find new opportunities,* some as Independent Director; some connections got me involved in very interesting innovative projects with the national education policy, and now, as part of the TiE community, we are working to host the TiE Global Summit 2024. Thus, networks can provide immense ***support and collaborative opportunities.***

v. Networks for Community and Social Impact

As I have mentioned in the earlier chapters, I have always been interested in ***social impact and community initiatives,*** both at an organizational and personal level. Being a senior international corporate leader, we were actively engaged in Corporate Social responsibility. I knew that I needed to have the right network for social / community initiatives where companies like mine would engage – for example, we would turn to the Big 4 consulting firms to see what they recommended. Yet I also knew that I had to build my personal network in this area as it was an area of my passion.

When I left Thomson Reuters, I left a lot of my professional networks associated with the company, yet the personal connections I made there enabled me to continue contributing to those communities long after my corporate stint. Hence, I believe that if you are interested in this sector, *build your personal connections. These networks provide friends and acquaintances with common aspirations, and they are essential for emotional well-being- and a sense of belonging.* They provide opportunities for social activities, hobbies, and personal relationships. Therefore, when I joined Social Venture Partners [SVP], it was taking the long view – I knew I had enough opportunities within my organization for Corporate Social Responsibility related initiatives, but my membership with SVP would enable me to dial up my engagement with the social sector when I left the corporate world.

vi. Networks for community development and resilience.

We are all part of civil society, and we engage in driving collective action [e.g., for Diversity and Equity Inclusion in business], responding to disasters [*most corporates had a strong Covid response unit not just for their employees but for the communities they engaged with*] and the sharing of resources and information in communities. [*again, Covid is a good example of how the community worked*]. I know I was involved in the company networks to help get hospital beds, ventilators, medicines, etc. I was also involved in the YPO forum groups and the local neighborhood, to just name a few.

There was constant information exchange as I was one of the common nodes.

Networks are also great places for getting input for **problem-solving, being engaged in influence and advocacy, mentorship or guidance, and even health and well-being.** I definitely leveraged the NASSCOM communities over the years, whether to deal with disasters or identify solutions for 'Patient funding for Deep Tech.'

vii. Networks as places for personal growth

All these networks support your personal growth. Look at your goals and see what kind of groups can support you in achieving these goals.

Ever since the INK events started in India, I have tried to attend them as I saw them as my brain spa! One can find different groups to nurture various facets of our being. During Covid, I joined a number of groups:

At a virtual water-painting class, I came across some lovely people. I have stayed in touch even after a few years- various business communities within YPOs who helped with business opportunities, self-growth, and wellness apart from Covid emergencies, which I have already mentioned.

Our office outreach programs, both within and outside the organization, are not just for Covid-related matters but also for continued education and mental well-being.

Family groups with whom we started with art appreciation and art classes, health and wellness programs, and I continue to do yoga virtually with them

All these groups nurture our overall well-being, which is the bedrock for our professional growth.

viii. Virtual Networks/Communities and On-line Presence

As I was leaving the corporate world, I was told by a younger colleague that I had no **Online Social presence** and, hence, no **virtual network** to leverage.

It was the tail end of Covid shutdowns, and it was important to get my LinkedIn profile updated and learn about the concepts of SEO [search engine optimization], etc., apart from setting up a basic website. I started writing at periodic intervals on my LinkedIn page.

Like the real world – we can build a *huge virtual network*, but is it *relevant?* Do we know how to leverage it for the larger purpose? Some of my early engagements with digital marketing gave me some perspectives. My years with the bank have made me cautious about what I say online. This is both an advantage and a challenge, as well as it makes me invisible in spaces where I may be able to contribute.

Communities such as LinkedIn, Instagram, Facebook, or other social media can be great tools for your business development and customer communities.

ix. Cross-Cultural and International Networks

Cross Cultural or International networks are important in today's globally connected world. Don't be afraid to experiment. I found myself saying yes to being an advisor to an Israeli startup. Having been part of global organizations for over 25 years, I missed the international interactions, and this fit into what I was now doing. This engagement not only gave me lots of learning, but it also made me a friend. It came to me through a LinkedIn meeting request, so just be open to opportunities!

For building cross-border business, it is important to understand how to leverage the international communities. Many will exist in your city. Find and engage with them.

3. Types of Networks
i. Professional, Personal, and Social Networks

Studies differentiate between professional and social networks, showcasing their unique roles in personal and career development. A few years before I left my corporate life, I was dealing with my father's aging and associated elder care. I was talking to a good professional colleague who had given valuable leadership advice in the past, so while talking about my career, I spoke about the pressures on the home front. She said, "S, if you go in asking for a role based on your personal needs, no one is going to take you seriously." This is after having been an MD for over 16 years! I was embarrassed, but later, I realized that career conversations need to be handled professionally.

The same topic can be shared within your family or friends' network, where you can lead the conversation on the challenges of elder care. In this forum, most will provide support and advice and make the individual the center of the conversation. This is a personal/social network. We keep learning through life.

In another situation, in the housing community where I live, I know a lot of women. We see each other when we are out for a walk/run or during community events. At one of these lunches, as I was talking to a few women, I realized that most of them had strong professional careers, such as Head of Architecture, CFO, etc. – people I was looking to recruit! Yet, we continued to engage as members of a social group and did not exploit that situation for a professional opportunity.

At the same time, I observed that the men in that event seemed to be comfortable co-mingling the conversation with professional and social topics. I consciously tried doing this after that experience, that is, trying to meet up for professional conversations. It has not been as successful as I would have liked, unlike in other formal spaces.

ii. Supportive Networks

Supportive networks are essential for our individual well-being, personal growth, and success.

- *Emotional support.* The day I had to sack someone for cause, I was devastated. It was my personal network that gave me perspective. My professional network gave me practical advice, including the one about the risks of "guilt by association," which enabled me to take effective preventive and corrective action for the long term.

- ***Encouragement and Motivation.*** I wasn't sure whether I could cope with elder care, and one of my professional friends said, "Don't worry, you will be able to figure it out." Maybe it was the way it was said – full of certitude and confidence. It gave me the confidence to carry on and not step off my career path. Leverage your personal board, as they are interested in you but are not too closely engaged with the issue.
- ***Professional development.*** Most business forums will have specialized programs that one can attend, which in turn can lead to job offers, promotions, and collaborations.
- ***Facilitate collaboration and resource-sharing.*** Most of my independent directorships came from referrals, after which they go through a process of selection.
- ***Collaborative Networks.*** This is true for many people who can find new market partners, suppliers, etc., through collaborative networks. We often hear stories of how business started in someone's bedroom or in another's office.
- ***Diverse networks*** generally provide varied perspectives, cultures, and ideas. This naturally sparks creativity and innovation. During the short time I had exposure to a group working on the Indian national education policy, I had the most amazing exposure to teachers from tribal schools and vice chancellors of universities and very popular city schools. It provided me with a significant understanding of the various challenges and opportunities facing the education sector. This naturally provides more chances for ***problem-solving with experts.***
- ***Networks for Health and Well-being,*** including in the professional arena, there is a growing community. Covid threw up the challenges of health, mental well-being, and

challenges to productivity. The startup community is building new ways to tackle this problem, often based on the personal experience of the founders and technology and communities.

- My YPO forum has provided me with a supportive network for well over 20 years, and I suspect it will provide **life-long friendships**. *It also provides* **resiliency when dealing with adversities.**

Supportive **networks need to be built and nurtured proactively like any other relationship.** *We need to take a long view.* A transactional approach is not very rewarding. I have known people for 10-15 years before I was tapped by them to contribute to a major program that I was interested in. It does not happen overnight or even when one is expecting something.

iii. Challenge Networks

We also need *networks that challenge us.* They are essential for personal and professional development. Similar to the supportive networks, the challenge networks also provide diverse perspectives and mentoring, which is often very direct and makes one confront one's blind spots. *Constructive feedback and innovative solutions come with the challenge process; these networks also provide challenging projects and opportunities.*

Many of the *startup accelerators/ incubators provide a challenging yet supportive community.* Being part of these groups is truly enriching. To get the most from this type of community, one needs to be actively engaged and participate in events and programs that are initiated by these forums.

I have been very fortunate to have had these networks, which have helped me at different stages of my career. Hence, *my advice is for people to go and build your tribes!*

Not all groups you want to be in will let you in; find the adjacency. As someone said, *if you are not invited to the table you want, create your own table.*

iv. Every Professional Network is different

As someone who straddles multiple professional networks, I learned a few things. *Even among professionals within a sector, there are nuances among the groups.*

When Thomson Financial and the Reuters market data team were being merged, one would have thought that culturally, it would be similar. The Thomson team was very focused on how the user would leverage the information to create financial value for themselves and, therefore, Thomson Financial. That was the DNA of the organization. For the same function, the Reuters team took their cue from the organizational culture that had evolved from news – which impacted and changed lives. When addressing the teams during the merger, we had to keep both these aspects in mind.

Financial services are bucketed together – I first realized how different the insurance and banking folks were when we got a new manager in Axa, who was from an American bank. He started with due diligence. The insurance team was upset as they operated based on trust.

Despite having been in financial services all my career, I realized that the FinTech folks are mainly Technology-driven, and a lot of the implicit understanding of bankers, especially around regulatory topics, is not natural for them.

Thus, while motivating different groups, it is important to draw up the persona of that team to understand how they operate.

Over the years, when addressing a town hall, I will start with a story, and depending on the crowd, I will style my presentation accordingly.

Example: Ops guys will want the punch line first. The Techies need a lot of data, analysis, and options before getting to the punch line. The Bankers want data and then the financial outcomes. Yes, I know this sounds stereotypical …yet this is just a simple way to illustrate *how to draw up your professional stakeholder personas.*

I often struggle when working with *NGOs. They work from the heart but may not always look at productivity/efficiency* as a way to get things done, look at the return on investments, or even know the various stakeholders to see if they are trustworthy. So, at the bank, when setting up the process for CSR, it was based on the same risk principles that we would use while making investments. This was tough for many of the NGOs working with us.

v. *Style of Engagement*

Different groups have their own 'language' of sharing information, the way they present it, etc. Geographic difference – e.g., the way I would *present to the American/UK team will be different from how it is presented to the German or Indian team. To be effective, it is important to understand the variance.*

I find the different functional groups are also very varied – for example, *quasi-academic-government networks have a certain formality in the way they engage compared to a startup or technology crowd.*

The *dressing* is more formal in government and senior business circles, though it is definitely relaxed in technology. So, *watch out for the underlying factors that drive a network*. Otherwise, one will blunder around.

For example, I had to learn that a startup network accepts that it will be more driven by its behaviors and immediate trends, whereas mature business forums tend to be more process-driven.

4. Understanding Networks
i. *Network Analysis*

Network analysis is a field of research that focuses on the structure and dynamics of networks. It provides insights into how information flows, who holds central positions, and how networks evolve over time. Consciously or unconsciously, we all gravitate toward the *'head honcho' in the network* when we join a new group. Even if you are shy, someone will prod you to go forward.

I was at the Thomson Senior Leadership Conference, and a good friend and a senior leader from HR told me to go and engage with the Board members. As she saw me react – she exclaimed, "I would never have realized that you are this shy!"

It was important for my team in India to have the support of various board members, which made me put aside my natural reticence and go forward and engage. *Understand the network and see what you need to do for the professional growth of your organization/self. Don't waste your energy on internal dialogues about your feelings of awkwardness – it is a waste of time.*

How does the information flow within the network? I had been a member of the NASSCOM community for over a decade when I ended up being on the National Exco ...the information that came to us was not something the average person got access to.

Around that time, I was at Thomson Reuters, and as a media entity, we had access to a lot of information. Hence, when I joined Deutsche Bank with its banking rules of *"Info on a need-to-know basis"* was a bit of a shock. Today, I make sure I have facts coming from feeds and also insights coming from varied networks of people, apart from evolving my own point of view.

Often, this makes me a valued resource in many groups.

ii. Information access and evolution

Earlier, it was about our access to information.

Today, with access to the net, we all have information, but do we know the special sites, thinkers, and groups to access?

With the AI revolution, what is still needed to set us apart? ...in the short term, we need to build our local language and micro LLMs to add to the global body of knowledge, but the future is evolving.

5. Quick Networking Hacks

i. Virtual Engagements

It works for me as they cut out the travel and also a lot of small talk. It *enables me to interact with people on specific topics.* For example, I often *reach out to people* whose writing or podcasts appeal to me and ask *for a 20-minute call.*

This is great as it's not too long. One can find out if one wants to follow up with more interactions. *Prepare yourself with* a perspective/information that you can share; have a set of questions that you want to ask the person.

ii. Seminars and Symposiums

This is a great way to meet subject matter experts. Further, one can build on collaborations more easily. It is for this reason I no longer like the very large events as it is difficult to meet all the people we want as well as listen to the speakers. *Smaller events enable you to engage across a wider spectrum of people.*

For example, at a small Quantum seminar, I met with students, academicians, business folks, and government functionaries ...

iii. Leveraging Large Group Events

Having said that, I will go to a very large event, such as the Global FinTech Festival, where over 50k people attend. *Prepare:* By identifying the sessions, people, and workshops you want to attend or meet. Sometimes, I find it useful to plan and join others who may have similar objectives ahead of the session. Thereby circumventing the challenges of the crowd or being overwhelmed.

iv. One-to-one and small group meetings.

Virtual meetings, lunch, dinner, and coffee are great ways to build depth for collaborations. Further, the smaller group sessions help build out the relationships more easily.

v. Special Networking days/evenings

I typically avoid weekend networking; it is only for family. I am now making exceptions, but it messes up with my schedule.

There are lots of networks, and it's important to understand what type of networks you are looking for. They can be business forums, specialist forums, startup forums, tech forums, etc. As we are focused on professional development, I am not going into other groups.

vi. Alumni Networks

Alumni **network** may also be a good place to explore. The risk I found with Alumni groups was that we spent too much time on nostalgic reminiscence!

vii. Learning Networks

Learning something new – whether it is training or workshops, effort is vital. It keeps us alive. If you don't have time, don't worry about it. It's okay not to network; instead, read a page a day, listen to a 10-minute podcast, and reach out to a specialist in the area of something that interests you. Maybe just subscribe to a WhatsApp group and **indulge in what makes you grow.**

viii. Strategies for Connecting

Before starting on any journey, understand **WHY** you want to engage with that network. I.e., ***set your goals.*** You can explore, but after a point, you need to be clear about what you want from that interaction. Is it helping you fulfill your overall agenda?

I was coming back from a conference, and I was with an entrepreneurial friend. We were discussing the sessions and the people we met and started kick-around some ideas. At the end of the plane ride, he said, "I got my return on investment for attending the conference." I realized I was measuring the effectiveness of the conference in very different terms: i.e., what was the new thing that I learned. I was measuring it in terms of learning while my friend was looking at revenue-generating business opportunities. It doesn't matter what you measure. Why *is it important to you?*

We have already spoken about *leveraging existing contacts, attending events and conferences, and joining professional forums, online forums, and Network mixers.* Explore and see if you can join a *volunteering group* if that interests you. Offer to help and support others in what they are doing, even if that is not your main goal. You will build allies.

The biggest challenge for us is to *follow up and stay in touch.* It could be an afternoon conversation without an agenda, or you could ask for advice/perspectives.

It is important to remain authentic. I go to some conferences to just listen to the speakers and not the network, while in others, it is just the opposite.

Recognize why you are doing it. Sometimes, *when I am exhausted, just listening to amazing speakers gives me inspiration.*

At the end of the day, networks are not just contacts but building meaningful and mutually beneficial relationships, and this takes time and effort. Consider your business goals and then explore the type of business network that will help you most effectively. Multiple forums can help, provided you have the bandwidth.

ix. *I am not very good at networking!*

This is a refrain that we often hear. We are caught up with our day job. Our family commitments make it difficult to take on a heavy load of networking. Worse, we are working across the globe, and networking is essential.

Yet, if this is needed for your goal, you have to find the most effective way to manage this. Don't make this your excuse.

6. Developing Healthy Boundaries

I remember some socially awkward events. I found that it was easier to get people talking about their childhood shenanigans. It got people going. This may not really be very appropriate in a work scenario. Ask people for their most fun work experience, most courageous, most complex, and most happy; it gets the ball rolling. Tugging the emotion will trigger a more effective mood. These are skills that often take years to develop, and even then, we make mistakes. In all relationships, boundaries need to be established. Some of us know this instinctively, yet in some situations, *we have to learn how to set boundaries*.

As you would have gathered, I go back to **self-awareness. Understand your needs, limits, and priorities,** and then see what **boundaries** you need to set along with **your values**. A typical investment bank crowd would work hard and party hard. Not being a drinker, these impromptu events would be an exercise in how long I could stay drinking a club soda without finding the restroom!

Yet the watering holes around Guardian Royal Exchange were the easiest way to meet with many of my colleagues whose calendars made it impossible to find time with them.

This worked for me when traveling. I rarely did this when I was at home.

We have all heard about the need to *Communicate Clearly* and *to express our boundaries to others in no unclear terms*. The challenge is when the other person is not willing to accept your stand. Here is when *the art of managing situations becomes helpful.*

Focus on the outcome you want. At one stage in my career, I had a fair amount of pressure to drink at social events. I tried to communicate clearly, respectfully, and assertively that my choice was a NO, but when it was becoming unpleasantly confrontational, and my boss shared that the perception that people would have of me would be that of a 'holier than thou' person, I decided that it was far easier to get a glass of whatever was there and hold onto it. People assumed that I was drinking, and it became a non-issue.

Maybe it was a lame approach, but it was a lot less energy-draining without too much drama. Today, I find it far easier to say NO with humor. Maybe I am older, stronger in my ability to say NO, or society is more accepting of people.

A few other things that I have learned are that you need to prioritize your well-being. *Say NO to anything that impacts 'you' negatively.'* The art of saying NO and setting your boundaries early is vital, and you should not feel guilty about it.

For example, *when negotiating a job*, explain why you will not work over the weekends if that is important to you, and then ensure you follow it up with action. Everyone will test your boundaries. One of the things *I learned is not to overexplain*, which I am prone to do. It is better to *keep it simple with a basic explanation*. In this context, one needs to be aware of manipulative behavior and have tactics to manage it.

I will often *delegate stuff* as I know it will help me *manage my time*. Yet one of my challenges has always been over-committing. So, once in a while, I will take stock and stop doing some things or change how I do other activities, including the use of technology. The usual best practices include leveraging schedules, prioritizing, avoiding checking mail messages, and getting distracted. The 4-Hour Workweek blogs by Tim Ferris have wonderful hacks to manage your time [5].

Setting healthy boundaries is a continuous process, and especially if you are making changes, it will take others some time to adjust to your new boundaries. You need to be firm and consistent to establish it. I reckon *it's a bit like training a puppy; you do need to say even when you are tempted to give in. You are both the puppy and the trainer!*

In more *formal networks*, the *guardrails could be confidentiality agreements, code of conduct and ethics, meeting etiquette, data privacy rules* [over and above the legal requirements], *conflict resolution, decision-making guidelines, membership criteria* for networks [e.g., interview process in many networks or financial cut-off, etc.], *non-solicitation policies and conflict of interest, guidelines for diversity, equity, and inclusion, behavioral guidelines around hate speech, time management, dealing with intellectual property*, etc.

While it may seem excessive, different forums will emphasize different elements strongly depending on their core objectives

Become aware of the written and unwritten rules and ensure they're aligned with your personal values.

7. Risks and Challenges of Networks

One of my bosses said, "S, *these networks are great. They will get you to take on more and more activities until it becomes a serious time waster and starts impacting your work and life*". It is, therefore, important to understand your appetite for the amount of time you want to engage in the networks. I have found that I will say yes to one activity, and it is often linked to 5 other activities that I was not aware of. It can be a time and energy drainer.

Networks give us access to a lot of people, yet not all of them are necessary for your primary goals. Many connections can be shallow and inauthentic, which is why the *quality of the network is more important than quantity.*

Also, as we engage with a lot of people, we will *lose a bit of our privacy*. Human interactions will come with *other challenges of conflicts, misunderstanding, peer pressure to conform, burnout, and risk of exploitation.*

Just as you assess if you have too much to do, *assess which of your networks really work for you.*

8. Research on Networking

Networking is a complex area of research, and it covers topics such as social connections, the anthropology of networks, and professional relationships.

Years ago, I had been asked to speak on networks, and my go-to book was Nicholas A. Christakis and James H. Fowler's book *"Connected."* [3]. One of the ideas from the book that stayed with me is the story of a number of schools getting affected by a certain behavior across schools in Africa – the idea of *social contagion* is explained in this study.

They speak about the ways ideas are spread and how behaviors and emotions are transmitted across social networks. The anthropological implications of networks left a deep impact on me.

I always have an image of a group of elephants in Masai Mara pushing a young male out of the group when it is time for him to leave them. It was so disconcerting; an hour before, he was part of the group, and then he wasn't. The evolutionary behavior of groups and networks are still areas of research, and I am not sure how they impact us even today.

i. Exploring Network Concepts

Organizations such as WEF, YPO, Rotary, Lions Club, and Freemasons have all emphasized the value of social connections in terms of access to resources, information, and opportunities.

An interesting adjunct to this is *Network Structure*, where concepts such as centrality, tie strength, and network density are evaluated to study the flow of information and how behavior is controlled. Recently, I shared that I am an independent director on LinkedIn.

A number of people have reached out to me to ask me how to get onto Boards. While head-hunters can find non-executive director positions, it is the networks that I am part of that have made it happen. The people who have referred me or asked me to reach out to the companies are key players in the network [centrality] and, hence, could help the decision-makers.

In recent years, there have been a lot of studies on the importance of diversity in driving creativity. Diverse networks and teams bring people from different backgrounds, perspectives, and capabilities together, and this leads to more robust and creative solutions. Yet, it is important to know how to handle diversity. At a country / societal level, there are a lot of discussions on how to engage and manage multicultural environments. In large international firms, this is an essential requirement, and some companies are better at it than others. One of my learnings was that apart from having a common vision and purpose, knowing how to execute also needs some harmonization for the network to operate effectively.

Less intense than the *economic networks are the professional and business networks, which are more about exchanging information about the latest trends, playing an advocacy role, or creating marketplaces* such as NASSCOM, SIIA [4], etc. The same is true of academic networks, the field of philanthropy, or social impact space. As I am building these networks, I realize that there are both subtle and big differences across these networks, similar to the business world.

Finally, *Social Online Networks* are very important today whether to position oneself for a job, business, or any other reason.

Usually, 1 percent is very active, another 9-10% engage occasionally, and the remaining 90% are just observers. In large platforms, these numbers are impactful. The SEO – algorithms are vital for marketing. It is important to understand the value of these kinds of networks to see how communication in these forums impacts relationships in the real world. I rarely went into LinkedIn until 2020. So, even though people have asked me to endorse them or asked for any engagement, my non-response meant that it impacted interaction in the real world. So, if you choose those forums to engage, establish a predictable engagement pattern.

The *psychological impact of our networks on our self-esteem, social anxiety, and personality are areas of serious discussion as they affect our well-being and mental health.*

All networks – physical or virtual, need to be nurtured and managed. At the end of the day, networks are made up of people, and we need to manage the relationships with each individual. Network ethics and norms need to be understood.

Just like how one can't play football with the rules of hockey, each network has its rules, and we need to understand them and know that if we want to be part of such a group, we must accept the values of that forum.

Rotary and Lions tend to have fairly structured hierarchies, whereas today's technology forums are more democratic, yet both need us to contribute actively.

As you go forward in your career, understand how you operate and what is needed for your professional career and growth ahead.

For example, if you don't want to talk to people but want to drive revenue for your company, you have to see what the best way forward is for you.

Overall, *research demonstrates the* **value of networks** *in various aspects of life, from career success to community resilience and well-being.*

The specific findings may vary depending on the context and the focus of the research, but they collectively emphasize the importance of cultivating and leveraging social and professional connections.

Scientific studies have linked social networks to better mental and physical health. Strong social connections are associated with reduced stress, improved emotional well-being, and even increased longevity. Research has also explored how networks influence decision-making by shaping opinions, affecting voting behavior, and impacting policy decisions.

Therefore, it is inevitable that your professional goals/development will be influenced by your networks.

If you have a network of people who are actively involved in conservation, even if you are not strongly motivated, you will get involved with these activities.

In summary, networks are essential for personal and professional growth, career advancement, knowledge acquisition, and emotional well-being. *Cultivating and maintaining these connections is like the lifeblood of a professional.*

Exercise:
1. *List the various networks that you are part of professionally and socially.*
2. *Write down what you contribute to the network.*
3. *Write down what you gain from the network.*
4. *Why are you in the networks?*
5. *What do you want from that network?*
6. *Do you know the key players within the network?*
7. *What is the frequency/plan of engagement with the network?*
8. *Do you want to draw up a stakeholder map for the networks against the*

goals that you want for yourself?
   9. What else do you want from this?
   10. See the gaps and then choose how you want to address them.

Conclusion:

Networks play a huge role in our professional success. Think about what you are doing to leverage this tool. By taking the time to reflect on the "why" behind our decisions, we gain a deeper understanding of our own motivations and goals, allowing us to align our actions with our purpose. This clarity not only simplifies the decision-making process but also helps us stay focused on what really matters, leading to greater productivity and satisfaction in our careers.

In this context, don't forget to examine how your networks support you. So, the next time you find yourself at a crossroads, take a step back and ask yourself, "Why?" - you may be surprised at the clarity and direction it provides.

6
THRIVING IN UNCERTAINTY

The Israeli start-up in which I was involved was looking at supporting gig workers in the global supply chain. When I first got involved, the 22-member teams operated from 15 countries, and I loved the international flavor and the collaboration of this multicultural group. When the Ukraine-Russian situation emerged, we thought it would be over within a short time. The GM was Ukrainian, and the team had to look at business continuity very seriously. Ultimately, the team had to pivot into sustainability and circular economy, given the geopolitical situation. This is not something we would have normally planned for while starting the business. Yet, we had to be flexible as factors beyond our control unfolded.

Life is full of change, which creates uncertainty. In response to that change, we need to be agile and adapt; we need to become resilient and build a growth mindset. These life skills are essential tools for our lives, both professional and personal.

Exercise:
Identify a list of changes you are currently dealing with:
1. Your professional life..
2. Personal relationships...
3. Your financial life..
For each of these changes, identify which ones made you feel:
1. Positive and...
2. Those that make you feel uncomfortable..........................
3. Identify any patterns that you recognize.........................
4. Any new insights that you have based on some of the earlier chapters

1. Uncertainty

All goals come with built-in uncertainty with regard to their success. Even with all the planning to drive change, external and internal factors will derail the journey.

As an entrepreneur, I know that only 4-6% of start-ups are truly successful, and there may be another ~15% who are reasonably successful. But the rest will fail. These are the odds going in.

To be the CEO or finding your dream job also has similar levels of uncertainty, especially as you get more senior or specialized.

This kind of uncertainty exists for artists, sports people, and most other fields.

To reduce the odds of failure, we identify the risks and put in place controls and mitigants to manage them. Yet unexpected events can completely derail us.

In the past, when society was mainly agrarian, the weather, pestilence, the markets, and the availability of labor were the drivers of uncertainty. Today, with industrialization and digitalization, where there is plenty of choice, there is still fear of job loss or being unable to economically fend for oneself in an effective way. According to WEF, a net share of over 20% of companies expect AI to add jobs rather than replace them, and job losses are expected to occur with the emergence of humanoid and non-humanoid robots. Yet there are other reports that put job losses from 300m to a billion due to AI over the years. What we can say with any confidence is that we do not know what the real impact will be in our professions due to AI and other technology changes. Most of the jobs that will emerge definitely do not exist today. Most people in a career will change at least six jobs in probably as many companies.

What that implies is that there is no certainty of achieving our goals due to a vast number of uncontrollable factors, and we need to embrace change. So, how do we Thrive in this Uncertainty?

2. Change

Change is ongoing. We need to accept this fundamental fact. Embracing *changes* often pushes us to *innovation and creativity.* Using the AI example given above, we can already see how people are using AI to write books, create art, and make films leveraging this new tool. Serious business research in drug discovery, academia, business excellence, etc., is also quickly evolving using generative AI.

3. Mindset to thrive in uncertainty

i. Embrace Uncertainty or Suffer!

Having gone through multiple organizational changes, every time I encounter it, *I love* **the** *uncertainty.* I never know if I will thrive, survive, or will need to cut my losses, but it is exciting. I think my early childhood made me more **Resilient.** Figure out how you can *develop this mindset like a muscle.* Obviously, there are stress management techniques – exercise, meditation, and mindfulness to handle the immediate pressure. Yet it is a *long-term mindset* where one has the certitude that one will land on one's feet.

ii. What is your safety net?

I remember one acupressure doctor telling me he has always kept a financial buffer for two years, and that gave him the confidence to take risks. When dealing with the future, we need to put in place a practical safety net, but ultimately, we need to have inner confidence.

Phrases such as **"when the going gets tough, the tough get going"** or **"one will never be given something which we can't** *handle,"* sound very real to me. Figure out what your 'mantra' is.

iii. The mindset to understand gradual vs. sudden change

As we grow in our careers, we take on more and more responsibilities until we are so busy that we have no time to learn something new or develop new competencies. This happened to a colleague of mine. He was hardworking and delivering, yet he found himself getting bypassed by a lot of less experienced people. He was so focused on doing the job that he did not realize that the world had moved and that he had not invested in building new skills. How does he respond?

Your company is taken over by a more technologically advanced, aggressive entity. Your organization's culture is not able to adapt to this change – this means a lot of people can not cope with the new reality. All the companies where I have undergone mergers, acquisitions, and integration have resulted in this type of disruptive change. This causes us to feel fear and uncertainty.

It is not easy to navigate, yet if we learn the skills, it can make us thrive.

iv. Waves of Change

I first understood the concept of the Waves of Change when Axa bought Guardian Royal Exchange.

First, the board and the CXOs changed, along with their goals, and slowly, the changes started impacting the middle management. As the new team came up with different strategies for growth, this was also slowly cascaded down.

In our personal careers, not only can we watch for signals from the company, but we can also see how the world is changing around us and see if we have an opportunity to take advantage of it.

For example, many people from the financial sector move to FinTech companies. Hence, if you are looking for a change, watch the larger space.

v. Speed of Change

The speed at which the changes occur is also important. AI has been in the works for a long time but started picking up speed in

2019, and by early 2023, it became a tool that every digitally literate person was attempting to use. Yet not all professions and businesses are using it extensively yet.

Accelerated: A Guide to Innovating at the Speed of Change[1] by Brian Ardinger and *Building Trust and Relationships at the Speed of Change [2] by Kathy Jourdain and Jerry Nagel-* these two books are great resources for exploring the implications of the speed of change.

Over the years, I developed the instinct to spot change within the organization and to adapt quickly to the new reality. Today, the reason I like working in the think tank is because one is looking at long-term changes.

4. Strategies for Embracing Change

Biology is an inspiration for handling change.

i. Bite the bullet [fight]

When dealing with a situation that demands action, do we act? It could be something fairly simple: A number of years back, I had taken a group of 25-30 managers for a team-building weekend.

The location was a camp on the bank of a river in a forest area. To get there, we were dropped off on a country road, and we had to take a forest trail by foot to the camp for a couple of kilometers. The camp organizers would pick us up from the drop-off point and then bring us back once we were done. In the afternoon, when we were returning back to town, we got to this drop-off point on the road, and we were waiting for the bus to pick us up. It was late afternoon, with dark clouds gathering, and there was no sign of the bus. As it was a forest region, the locals warned us to get back to the main road as there was the risk of wild animals such as leopards and elephants. So, when a local bus turned up, we just hopped onto it and got to the nearest town. It was just Confront and Act.

A more complex situation could be when one is being harassed at work. One often sees individuals who do not want to confront the situation. They let it slide until it became a serious issue. We had a situation when a senior leader tended to be a micro-manager to the point of harassment. This was definitely not healthy when the rest of the people reporting to her were also senior. This caused significant attrition, and the board called out poor management as the reason for letting her go.

Face the change head-on and deal with it.

ii. Dip your toes and immerse yourself slowly [freeze?]

When the water is cold, we can immerse ourselves slowly by first dipping our toes. For example, in a new situation, we can sometimes freeze or take it gently. When building out a large technical solution, we would often start with a proof of concept, which would then progress to a pilot, and then finally, the final build, which would go live with one region, one product at a time. As a result, it can take years for a full roll-out.

In the start-up world, we often see people testing out a concept and then engaging with Beta customers to see Minimum Viable Products before growing the plans.

When we join a new group, we don't know the dynamics and the 'rules of engagement.' In this situation, we will test the waters to see how people respond and slowly build from there.

Acclimatize yourself to the change and then start acting.

iii. Run the other way [flight]

Sometimes, we know that a particular option is not a good fit. It could be a business partner, supplier, or even a customer or employer. Don't be afraid to walk away from something that doesn't feel right. I have often said no to job offers if it doesn't feel right.

After leaving the corporate world, I was asked to run a company as a partner while putting in a small amount of the capital. It was a good offer, but not the right fit for me as I was not keen on an operational role. Understand if you want to walk away from an opportunity or situation.

With some changes, it is ok to step away!

5. Practical Approaches to Handling Change
i. Information is Vital

To manage change effectively, one needs to be on top of the information that could affect your profession or organization. If you are building a product in the financial sector, then you need to always look out for new regulations. This happens a lot in the FinTech sector when the central regulators make changes, e.g., to lending norms in terms of risk ownership.

We know that in the banking sector, RSA standards are going to change by 2038, and if one is building a major infrastructure in 2028, then one would need to keep tabs on the new standards that need to be incorporated.

Most technology companies know that they need to keep on top of the changing technologies. Hence, the culture of these organizations is one of **learning and growth.**

In fact, the recruitment in these companies will look for this trait. If you are either working in these firms or want to build such a company, it is vital to have this as a value/behavior in your organization.

ii. Transparency: Open Communication

Open Communication enables us to **get the support** we need, especially during change.

I had shared how I was going to move ahead after my corporate career, and as a result, I had people providing me with ideas on what I could do.

They connected me to others. Don't be afraid to be open and vulnerable about the changes you are dealing with.

iii. Play the long game

While we have already spoken about professional **goal setting**, sometimes we don't know what to do next. For me, every time my organization was going through a merger, I never knew what would happen to my role.

The only goal I could have was to ensure that my team survived well and that individuals who were negatively impacted were supported to find roles outside the organization.

It was not always possible. Yet in all this, my personal journey was generally unclear – sometimes, I survived for a short while, and at other times, I was collateral damage. Yet my **professional purpose** was to have a fulfilling career, and these experiences enabled me to grow – *the long game was what I was playing.*

iv. *"Eat the Elephant – or maybe the pie! – and stay the course."*

Long back, I was putting in place a time-management plan, and the program had something called *"eat the elephant."* Over the years, multi-year change programs would kick off, with the senior leaders setting off the agenda for the change that was being planned. This would then have a cascade of communications across the organization at every level and region. In the meantime, changes would start from the strategic plan getting operationalized to execution – i.e., breaking it into smaller, manageable steps. This is true for personal changes as well – *break the activity into smaller chunks, schedule* it, and stay on course while adjusting for any unplanned situations that affect the plan.

v. **Set intentions and visualize success**

When we set intentions and visualize success, it is a call to both our conscious and subconscious minds to focus on the outcome we are after. I have found that this makes me more alert to all the changes that are happening and it makes me more nimble in responding to ongoing changes.

Often, before going into a tough meeting, I will set my intent for the outcome. I will work through various scenarios and will often use my team to play out various possibilities. So, I will be as prepared as I can be. Yet, I will leave myself open to what happens in the meeting rather than setting it up rigidly.

Our objective is to thrive in uncertainty – these are some tools to stay in control. Don't be too caught in the how, but keep the what and why harmonized. These techniques help one become more effective with all the changes in the professional journey.

6. Impact of Change on Individuals

Having gone through multiple organizational changes, from mergers and acquisitions to annual re-organizations, I have a first-hand understanding of the *impact of change on individuals.* It is profound – there is immense pressure; if one is on the exit path, it is traumatic.

Often, the sensitivity with which it is handled also scars us, even if we are impacted. A friend of mine in NY got so paranoid that he used to start hiding if he saw HR on his floor! Even the *period of uncertainty is very stressful.* Often, change will necessitate *learning new skills,* which are useful in the long term.

These changes can *impact career trajectories* – I have found there is a short-term impact and a longer-term impact. During a merger, some people lose their jobs in the first round if there is a duplication of roles. Others may survive this, but about 18-24 months later, they may find that their roles, which were vital during the change, are no longer relevant. So, in a corporate career, we need to handle these waves of change that impact our us.

Work-life balance becomes a myth during periods of change. Therefore, it is important to understand the various threads of life that one is handling at that point. **Workplace relationships** will definitely change. Some of the best colleagues who have to go into survival mode may not be able to have your back the way they used to, and others with whom you did not have such a great rapport may become your best buds! **Personal growth** will definitely happen, but it might come at the cost of one's **well-being**. Being aware of these elements will enable one to navigate change more proactively.

As a person who is instigating this change, be conscious of these factors as you work through your new professional goals. This type of change will be stimulating up to a point. After that, it can become stressful. For me, writing the book has been stressful from a time-management perspective.

7. Response to Change: Agility & Adaptability

Agility and adaptability are crucial responses to managing change. Some characteristics of agility and adaptability include *rapid response to change.* If, as an individual, you are agile and adaptable, you can handle personal growth more rapidly, which can support career advancement and reduce stress. It also *builds a mindset for constant problem-solving.* Both as an organization and as an individual, these traits and approaches enable us to build a competitive edge by becoming more innovative in meeting one's personal and organizational goals. In today's fast-paced, ever-changing world, these skills are vital for success. As a change leader, looking at some of the reasons behind the way people operated was a vital skill. *If you want to lead change, get familiar with frameworks that can help you.*

During the 2008 financial crisis, we had to constantly watch the markets and the organizations to ensure that our market data was relevant in the uncertain and complex world of international finance. Many of us have gone through the dot.com days and are part of today's start-up environment. The start-up ecosystem has been euphoric, yet it's getting tempered with strong financial prudence today. These boom-and-bust cycles teach us crisis management as well as how to be competitive. It can also lead to burnout. With the financial regulators getting very active post-2008, it has been an intense ride for anyone in the financial sector. Yet the opportunities that we have witnessed in countries like India with the India Stack, UPI, and basically *'Tech for Public Good'* have been transformational.

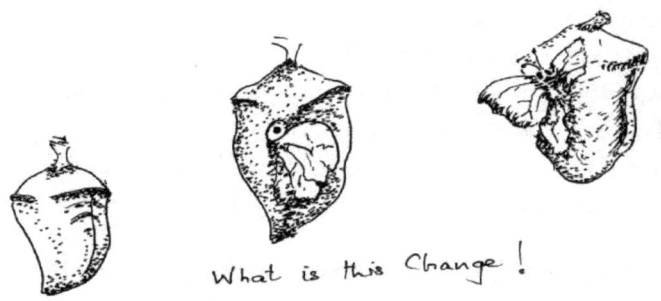

What is this Change!

i. Agility

Agility involves our ability to respond quickly and effectively to changing circumstances, and the decision-making needs to be rapid, capitalizing on emerging trends and addressing unforeseen challenges.

An experience from my work life was in 2008 when the financial crisis was spiraling quickly out of control. Every weekend, boards met to see how to handle the situation. As a team providing financial information to the markets, we had to respond very rapidly.

If I were a decision-maker in one of the affected institutions, it would have constant triage and action. Some of the individuals who got caught in this were alert enough to take care of their financial needs, while most were caught in a serious situation.

Going back to the Israeli start-up that I was advising, when the Ukraine war started, it was people first, as a number of employees were from the affected regions. As the CEO told the GM – if you hear that the soldiers are moving in your direction, run to the nearest European nation for shelter. As time went by, it became obvious that the global supply chains were impacted. Large European companies had to let go of their Russian contract workers. This impacted the gig economy.

In recent years, Agile methodology, a project management approach that involves breaking down the project into phases and emphasizes continuous collaboration and improvement, starts with meeting, planning, designing, developing, testing, and evaluating and goes back to meeting again to improve on the first cycle.

Agile decision-makers can adjust their strategies quickly, and there is significant **flexibility** in the way they absorb new information and use it for new solutions. As agile teams constantly look both internally and externally, they tend to ***identify risks*** fairly quickly and **address them**. *The agile approach embraces uncertainty as its base and, hence, is comfortable going with an iterative approach to decision-making.* This approach also fosters experimentation and **the emergence of innovation** in response to both internal and external changes. *Constant adaptation leads to* **learning orientation** *through* **scenario planning** *and resilience through understanding setbacks and through a process of constant improvement.* We see this in most companies that are leading with cutting-edge technologies.

So, if you are in one of these industries, check if you have built this muscle for yourself.

As the head of Business Engineering, this was one of the tools that we deployed for organizational change. I find that it is easy to change the process but much harder to change the human mindset. I also found it was a good method along with SCRUM to build a project, I.e., try, and if it fails, we fail fast and move ahead.

ii. Adaptability

Adaptability is all about our capability to handle our behavior in the face of changing environments, both internal and external. As decision-makers, we need to be open to new information and feedback and then change the choices we have already made. Being flexible like the willow – i.e., we bend but not break. I found this very useful during mergers and integration.

When Guardian Royal Exchange was bought by Axa, the Indian team of seventy people was not even a blip on their radar.

Many of our teams globally and regionally were changed – the regional audit team was moved to Singapore, the risk advisory business was sold, the India CEO was retiring, and his remit of oversight over the countries he managed was no longer with India. That left only the off-shored team. That year, I had nine bosses and had to go to the UK board six times asking for funding to grow. It was truly a time to adapt to ensure the team survived.

I have also found that my career has gone in cycles. I completed the tasks for the merger; then, I got into strategy, which was a more introspective role. I then moved into managing a company again. These cycles of intense growth followed by slower times seem necessary to internalize the learning that one experiences. This gives you great adaptive skills.

8. Response to Change: Resilience and Growth mindset
i. Resilience

Resilience is one of the most important qualities we need to develop to cope in the modern world. It is ***our ability to bounce back after setbacks and failures.*** I found the traders in the investment bank had the best temperament for this – they handled the profits and losses of their trades and didn't let it get them down. When they had losses, they were able to compartmentalize their feeling and stay focused on their actions. Of course, there are downsides to this quality, which we saw across the globe during the financial crisis.

All of these involve a mindset of **risk management**, *and decision-makers build it into their approach by building options for how they operate.* Having worked in financial services, risk management, and business continuity is deeply engrained in the way one works. We all saw this during Covid – international banks needed to ensure we operated without any downtime. Most of us had the traders and other front office teams working from home – a situation none of us would have envisaged before Covid. When one operates with a *long-term perspective,* one is able to look at short-term challenges and deal with them.

Resilience – the secret sauce! Or is it Post Traumatic Growth?

I have often been told that I am very strong and that I seem to handle anything that comes my way. I know how I feel; while I may not always be strong, I am resilient.

What does that mean? It means that I respond to adversity by coping, adapting, and dealing with setbacks, trauma, significant life changes, and sources of stress. It's not just 'bouncing back' but dealing with the aftermath of the adversity and growing through the experience. One truly lives to fight another day.

Hence, I like the *Post Traumatic Growth [PTG] theory, which explains this kind of transformation following a trauma. Upside: The New Science of Post-Traumatic Growth* [3] by Jim Rendon and *Post Traumatic Growth* by Brenda Ungerland [4] are two books I found very interesting. There are a number of YouTube programs from credible sources as well.

Almost all of us have had to deal with life's big and small problems. The Buddhists call it the suffering of the world. We have all lost dear ones, from grandparents, parents, and children to friends.

We have had to deal with illnesses both our own and as caregivers or of close relations being ill and feeling our utter helplessness in the face of it. We have had setbacks while studying and at work, some small and sometimes job losses which deplete us emotionally and financially. Yet, what keeps us going?

ii. Five Stages of Grief

When I fell ill, I am not sure if I truly went through the five stages of grief: denial, anger, bargaining, depression, and acceptance.

I definitely did not want to accept that I was ill as I was still very active. I did not acknowledge anger, so that may need to be addressed. I definitely bargained about not wanting to go for treatment.

Yet I had to get into action almost immediately, so my way of acceptance was to ask what treatment I needed; I also told the doctors that I did not want to know the stats and all the other details. I just wanted to get it dealt with. I tried to get on with my life at the office while being pragmatic about what needed to be done for my physical health. I was truly grateful for all the support I had – people, work, and finances. So I got involved with funding poor patients, volunteering to help the hospital and doctor with building websites, marketing, etc.

iii. Growth mindset

As I was thinking about this topic, I came across an interesting TEDx Christchurch talk by Dr.Lucy Hone, who spoke about her personal tragedy of losing a child. She had worked with the US Army to build resilience as a competence. When she was at the receiving end of all the professional support, she turned her back on a number of things and focused on HOPE.

iv. HOPE is fundamental

For me, the phrase of hope was, "If my soul has a purpose in life, I will get through this." Anything that shores up this hope was what I wanted. The reason I did not want medical statistics was that it talks about some percentage (%), and it is frankly irrelevant since you may be in the minority or majority. Recently, I was talking to a friend who spoke about her husband, who had to get five stents put for his heart to function. The doctor shared that they could provide a five-year guarantee for the stents. They went ahead with the procedure. As the five years came to an end, the sense of anxiety was intense; the doctor did a review and said that all was well, and five years later, he is still going strong.

v. 'Shxt' / Stuff happens

According to Dr Lucy Horn, resilient people tend to accept that adverse things will happen, and they just accept it and deal with it without wasting time on 'Why me'?, "How did it happen?,' etc. Recently, while working with a team on Assistive technology for people with disability, I was told that cancer is also considered a type of disability. I was taken aback and told the team that I had never realized that I was disabled! One of the interns working there wanted to understand why people get cancer, as her mother had got this disease. My reaction when she spoke to me was, "Why not?" Based on today's statistics, more than 60% are likely to get this illness and a significant number of them will be treated and get on in life We need to accept that these kinds of things will happen. In the workplace of today, research shows that in a 30–40-year career, there is a statistical probability of losing one's job 3-4 times. If these are the odds of life, we just need to acknowledge that this might happen to us and **accept it.**

Post the trauma, we will have a lot of stress. We will need to *focus on what needs to be addressed* and not see a problem everywhere. In the modern world, we are told that various life events impact our mental health. As Dr. Lucy Horn dealt with the loss of her child, she was told by very well-meaning people/professionals that there was a significant chance of divorce/ relationship breakdown in 5 years, depression, and mental health issues.

In such a situation, what does one choose? In my case, I chose treatment and living my life as normally as I could. At work, except for my boss and one or two others, people were not aware of the seriousness of my ill health. They just knew that I needed to take a few days off once in a while. I had a close circle of people who gave me positive strength – prayer and a sense of being loved. The rest did not matter. This ability to *focus on the longer term is what helps us operate in resiliency.*

I used to always *look for the positive/hunt for the positive*: what made me happy and grateful was looking at all those who were helping me. This was the doctors, the nurses, and at work, the close team that stepped in and supported us as we grew the team. Whether at work or elsewhere, I realized one needs *pragmatic positivity*. One cannot live in our imagination. One needs to acknowledge the reality we are dealing with, but after that, one can focus on the potential positive outcome. During Covid, we saw this in action.

Yuval Harari, a true futuristic thinker and historian, talks about resilience as one of the most essential competencies for the current world.

Technology will disrupt our lives in ways we don't know, with imminent job losses. Our family structures are changing dramatically due to various reasons, including the social media and digital world. We need very strong adaptive and coping strategies – from building psychological strength, positive and growth mindsets, building emotional regulators, cultivating high self-efficacy, which motivates a person to action, and most important of all, social support and establishing an ability to interpret challenges as opportunities for growth rather than obstacles. Past experiences can make you more resilient if appropriate support has been received. Today, we are also fortunate to have a resilience training program that promotes positive psychological traits, including neurosciences, which are looking at ways to improve this competence.

Given that we will deal with trauma, it is vital to build the coping skills and emotional fortitude to handle it. Throughout history, human civilization has been able to survive immense challenges. We need to internalize the skills at an individual level to take control of our lives.

vi. Growth mindset – some more perspectives

During the early years of my career, my director would always ask me what I was learning. Irrespective of whether the situation was positive or negative, this was the consistent question. Every task, from the mailroom work to filing and learning how the business functioned, brought learning. I learned that when I put in my effort, I could shift my abilities. For example, I like conceptual and abstract thinking, and I don't like detailed work. During a psychological assessment, my MBTI personality type [5] indicated that I am an ENTJ person – i.e., it confirmed my preference. Yet, as someone working in the financial sector, I had to build my muscle in working with details. This is now a strong part of me.

Today, *neurosciences call this neuroplasticity, and it is believed that the 'brain can change through deliberately focused bouts of learning.'* I really like this, as it gives us all hope that with effort, we can change. I came across a study by Dr Alia Crum, Professor of Psychology at Stanford University. She talks about neuroplasticity as being *the opposite of a Fixed mindset.* Another study that I enjoyed in this context was by *Dr. Carol Dweck, Professor of Psychology at Stanford University, who has done extensive studies around the 'Growth mindset.'* [6] You can listen to Dr Huberman and Dr.Alia Crum[7] discuss this topic in a way that you and I can use to build our growth mindsets.

Let me share some of my experiences to illustrate my understanding of this topic. When I was in the 3rd grade, I moved to a new school, and during this process, I missed 2 out of the four quarters. I was able to catch up with most subjects.

For math, I attended the tutorials during the lunch hour. By the time I got to the tutorial, after eating lunch, I had time to pick up the concepts but did not have enough practice time.

So, without adequate practice, I always felt that I was not good enough.

Unfortunately, I got decent grades, so I did not realize what I could do to improve my sense of inadequacy. This feeling of not being good enough in math followed me through school and into my job in financial services. Fortunately, financial calculators and computers were my compensating strategy – I understood the concepts, so it worked out.

Today, my interest in Quantum Science is supported by my belief that I can understand concepts but not math! The *fixed mindset still* exists.

Was I told that I was bad at math and yet told I was good with the concepts? ***Did I think*** I was bad at math but good at the concept? When I actually work with numbers, am I good [or bad] at it, and why? *What made me decide that I was not good at math? Psychologists ask us to explore which of these stories make us.*

I think I did not spend time practicing math initially because I spent my lunch hour playing. My parents initially believed that I was staying back late in school to catch up on my subjects. When they realized that was not the case, I was made to get home on time. Getting reasonable grades meant that no one understood the sense of insecurity I felt about the subject. As I got older, I put in just enough effort to get the grades I wanted, and I continued with my insecurity.

Once I got to work, I had to deal only with numbers, and it became second nature, yet the old sense of discomfort continued.

According to the research, the specific 'feedback' we get sends us down a certain path. What I find fascinating with this research is that *when praise is given for one's identity [aka. Intelligence], it can undermine motivation.* Whereas *feedback linked to effort [verbs to describe] makes one believe that with effort, we can improve and grow.*

Another example of this could be, "You are a great leader."

While this praise is nice, it also makes one insecure and fearful of failure. Yet if one receives specific feedback, "You provide clarity of purpose and discuss how it can be executed through the goals set. You also spend time working through how the individual can tackle this goal", it will propel one forward with a growth mindset.

As I left the corporate world, *I tried to drop the various identities associated with that world – a.k .a. "Managing Director, Banker, ...".*

Today, my best descriptor is Strategic Advisor, whether my identity is that of an independent director, distinguished professor, or consultant. Sometimes, it is very difficult to drop one's identity as it is linked to one's title, which is how the world recognizes you, to attaching one's identity to effort, which is what a true growth mindset is about. A growth mindset is highly relevant in the context of change, agility, adaptability, and resilience. This mindset, as proposed by psychologist Carol Dweck, is the belief that one's abilities and intelligence can be developed through effort, learning, and perseverance.

Conclusion:

Career transformation is a process, and it will come with lots of curved balls. The uncertainty can derail us unless we proactively respond.

There are people who believe we should have systems vs goals. My belief is we need to have *a purpose, a vision, and a mission towards which we progress.*

The path to reaching one's goals and purpose comes with many options, and the process of choosing is complex. Tools, one's temperament, networks, and approaches to change all play a role. The Frog and Toad children's book series by Arnold Lobel is a beautiful illustration of life. Go read it or watch a TV series [8]. One of the stories talks about the toad sowing the seeds for his garden and trying many things as he believes the seed is afraid to grow. The seed finally grows!

7
PURPOSE: YOUR BEDROCK TO "CHANGE"
P-GROW 2.0

Purpose should normally be in the beginning. I have deliberately kept this topic close to the end, as many of us are not sure of the purpose of our lives. There are exceptions, like those with a vocation *[to be a doctor, teacher, or a public service official]*, or maybe a passion *[like artists]*.

Given this, I thought it was prudent to focus on the first section - on setting professional goals, the adjacencies that impact them, and values that drive our actions – they are tangible and familiar.

I also explored how to choose and decide through increased self-awareness and the people we surround ourselves with.

Let us now pause to see if there is something higher than our goals that impacts our choices.

1. Purpose

As a young person, my goal was to become an army doctor and

be trained at the Armed Forces Medical College, [AFMC] Pune – it was very specific. I wanted to be like my dad, an army doctor who had taught at AFMC for a couple of years. When I was in middle school, I often used to go see him at the college, and he would indulge my curiosity by sharing the history of medicine. Over the years, I have accompanied him to the hospital while he visited his patients in the ICU [intensive care unit]. The sounds and beeps of the instruments in a dark room with just a few lights are still real to me. When the time came, I applied to a number of medical schools, yet I was interested in only this college.

Out of a hundred thousand people who applied that year, I was ranked sixteen and was one of those twenty girls in a batch of one hundred and twenty students. I was very happy. I then went for my army medical boards to get my fitness clearance.

Sometime between the medical boards and the few days before leaving, I had a serious epiphany. I knew I would be a good doctor, but I was not sure what the profession would do to me. I felt that I would either become immune to human suffering or would get overwhelmed by it. So, I made the hard choice to say NO to something that had driven me ever since I was a child.

I dropped that dream, but I had no idea what I wanted to do next. I just knew I needed to be economically independent. Economic independence meant freedom to live my life on my terms-whatever that meant!

2. Purpose vs Goal

As I examine that phase of my life, I am not sure I understood the implications. In my gut, I knew it was not the right direction for me. I listened to something inside of me. Even now, when occasionally I have had to take my dad to the military hospital, my mother will bring out this story and say, "S should have been an MD in this hospital, but it's ok she is still an MD!"

I had no specific goal, so I continued to study with the belief that it would enable me to get a job. I think my profession felt like a means to an end: *Freedom of choice.*

Years later, I recognized that there are a number of factors that drive me professionally – simply put, I like to be part of the Alpha team and want to strive to be my best.

I like the big picture and the fact that I may impact something bigger than myself. The paths may vary, but the goal had to have these components. These were some of the attributes of my purpose.

3. Evolution of Purpose

I am not sure how far one goes in search of Purpose. Biology, with its intense drive to survive, encompasses the fundamental purpose of life: to grow and to evolve. The evolution of humans has led us to different roles, from hunter-gatherers to farmers to the current society. The ancients show us life in those times through rich rock art, and the ancient scriptures show us a thriving imagination that goes well beyond survival. There is almost a constant yearning for more.

In the last few millennia, religion has shaped the human worldview and what one should strive for even more than our day-to-day lives.

The evolution of civilization and appropriate societal values and behaviors stem from this. The separation of church from state, the European colonization of various parts of the globe, the Industrial Revolution, Marxism, and, more recently, Information Technology with the internet, social media, and digitalization have all made the hold of religion recede.

Today, we have the full spectrum, from those who still have a clear purpose driven by spirituality or religion. There are those who believe *"Mathematics is the language of God"* and turn to sciences, economics, and culture. There are more and more people who are trying to find their passion and purpose and align it with their professional lives.

There are others who believe that life is perfect as it is and that we don't need to hunt for anything outside.

4. A few of My Explorations for Purpose

I came across Dan Millman's book *"The Way of the Peaceful Warrior"*[1] and quickly followed up with a number of his books like "The Journeys of Socrates," and "Living with Purpose". What I found fascinating was the protagonist, who is an Olympic gymnast who receives life lessons from a person at the gas station. These perspectives were very practical yet very introspective.

When I came across his book *"The Four Purposes of Life,"* [2] I was very taken. It speaks about learning one's life lessons and finding one's career and purpose through dealing with everyday challenges and making wiser decisions in the context of one's career and relationship.

The book talks about 12 life lessons that we need to go through and how this reveals our calling. Despite valuable insights and wisdom, this book, unlike his earlier works, did not resonate with me.

One of the quotes from the book by Leo Rosten has stayed with me, *"I think the purpose of life is, above all to matter, to count, to stand for something, to have made some difference that you lived at all".*

Many of us have done the exercise: What do you want to be remembered for, or what should your obituary say when you die? What is the legacy that you want to leave behind?

Michael Singer's *"The Surrender Experiment: My Journey into Life's Perfection"* [3] appealed to me profoundly as Michael Singer talks about a way of life that is very familiar to many Buddhist and Hindu practitioners -i.e., to surrender to life, come what may.

There are a lot of formal theories and concepts with regard to purpose-driven individuals and organizations, and my take is they all help, yet it has to be a personal or organizational quest. All 'how-to' approaches are limited.

We have touched on *Ikigai,* the Japanese concept earlier— identifying what you love doing, what you are good at, what the world needs, and what you are likely to be paid to do. This is a good way to approach your professional purpose.

In recent years, I read Simon Sinek's *"Start with Why"*[4], where he talks about having a strong sense of purpose to inspire action. During the Thomson Reuters merger, I found that having a shared vision and purpose helped us move forward rather than cling to our past identities of being a person from Thomson or Reuters. Yet, the period of adjustment is always rough.

Viktor Frankl's *"The Will to Meaning"* is a foundational book on Logotherapy [5]. As a holocaust survivor and psychiatrist, he believed that the search for meaning was a fundamental human drive that helps individuals handle adversity and find purpose. In his book, "*Viktor Frankl Recollections: An Autobiography,*" he says," I see beyond the misery of the situation to the potential for discovering a meaning behind it, and thus to turn an apparently meaningless suffering into a genuine human achievement. I am convinced that, in the final analysis, there is no situation that does not contain within it the seed of meaning. To a great extent, this conviction is the basis of Logotherapy (p.53)."

There are theories such as '*Self-determination theory*,' '*Sustainable and Socially Responsible Business*,' '*conscious capitalism*,' and '*positive psychology.*' These are great frameworks to operate from, yet they do not resonate with me on a deeper level. For me, even the belief that *"You are perfect as you are and don't need to change"* is just as good, for it is a *message of hope for people who are struggling.*

A quote I read when I was in school, *'My soul is an adventurer in life,'* is what resonates most with me. I find most joy in experiencing new things and learning. Every time I pick up something, it feels like a piece of the magnificent puzzle of creation. That is more my purpose, and the detours in life are part of this discovery.

From a professional perspective, last year, I felt that I only wanted to get involved in efforts that created Abundance in terms of time, energy, or wealth. Thus, start-ups were a good place. I have rejected a number of offers for Independent Directorships, yet I picked those that made me believe that I could support the growth and transformation OR the business was driving Impact and Sustainability. Educational institutions and think tanks have the ability to influence people for further metamorphosis. In most cases, I may not create Abundance for myself, but in the larger scheme of things, it supports growth, change, and evolution.

During the writing of this book, I saw that there are multiple wars going on in the world, and it is difficult to make sense of these horrific situations. Talking about our mundane life choices seems almost trite. Yet, it is important to frame one's life purpose so that it can help us navigate the various twists and turns of our life journey. This is the superset from which we can operate.

5. Inspirational Quotes from Recent History

Mahatma Gandhi: "My life is my message." Gandhi's purpose was to inspire people in India to join the freedom struggle through non-violent approaches. This has inspired movements for civil rights and freedom worldwide.

Nelson Mandela: "I have cherished the ideal of a democratic and free society in which all persons live together in harmony and with equal opportunities." Mandela was fighting apartheid, and he worked towards a free, democratic, and racially equitable South Africa.

Martin Luther King Jr.: "I have a dream that my four little children will one day live in a nation where they will not be judged by the color of their skin but by the content of their character." Dr. King advocated civil rights and equality for African Americans through non-violent activism.

Marie Curie: "Nothing in life is to be feared, it is only to be understood. Now is the time to understand more so that we may fear less." Marie Curie worked to advance scientific knowledge, particularly in the field of radioactivity, despite facing significant challenges as a female scientist and received 2 Nobel prizes.

Steve Jobs: "Your work is going to fill a large part of your life, and the only way to be truly satisfied is to do what you believe is great work. And the only way to do great work is to love what you do."

Most of us struggle to articulate what drives us. Yet, it is worth trying to understand it.

Like everyone, I have also been experimenting with Generative AI. I am sharing some of the purpose statements that I got from ChatGPT.

- ***Mission-driven Purpose Statement:*** "My purpose is to empower people to reach their full potential through improved access to education especially in underserved communities."
- ***Passion-Centric Purpose Statement:*** "I'm driven to create art that evokes joy and introspection through a deep emotional connect with people."
- ***Values-Oriented Purpose Statement:*** "My purpose is to foster a better world for future generations by living a life of honesty, empathy, and environmental stewardship."
- ***Legacy-Focused Purpose Statement:*** "I aim to leave a lasting legacy of kindness and compassion, positively impacting the lives of those I encounter."
- ***Growth and Learning Purpose Statement:*** "My purpose is to continuously learn and grow, embracing challenges as opportunities for personal development."
- ***Health and Wellness Purpose Statement:*** "I am dedicated to nurturing my physical and mental well-being, setting an

example for others to lead healthier lives."
- **Community and Social Impact Purpose Statement:** "My purpose is to contribute to my community's welfare, working towards social justice and equality."
- **Entrepreneurial Purpose Statement:** "I'm driven to create innovative solutions to address pressing global challenges, fostering sustainable progress."
- **Family-Cantered Purpose Statement:** "My purpose is to provide unwavering love and support to my family, nurturing their growth and happiness."
- **Spiritual or Faith-Based Purpose Statement:** "I find purpose in deepening my spiritual connection and living in alignment with my faith's principles."

While these are good statements, the purpose, as demonstrated by real people, appeals to me more. It is based on a deep understanding of what drives us and is shaped by our life experiences. Our personal purpose may evolve over time, and it's okay to revise and refine it as we grow.

There is a part of me that recognizes that I get tremendous joy in decoding the world. It is as though I have found another piece of the puzzle that is part of creation.

6. Goals and Purpose inter-twined

We have spent the entire first section of the book on goals; they serve a different role and are distinct from purpose.

I think of Goals as being specific, measurable, achievable, and time-bound, which we can classify as done or not done. They have concrete outcomes when we work towards them with an endpoint. They may fulfill our larger purpose or vision.

Meanwhile, *Purpose* is much broader and refers to the deeper reason why we exist or what drives us. It *is the 'why' of who we are and what we do.* As it is a superset, it can help with our choices and actions and deal with situations that derail us from our goals.

In a way, goals are steps on the way to living and achieving your purpose. Purpose provides the direction, while goals are the milestones. This is a deeper and more philosophical journey, and sometimes, we may want to just focus on the goals.

A few weeks back, I was mentoring a young woman with her start-up. Soon, it became a conversation for a life coach. She had to think about her start-up journey in terms of how her parents saw her, her relationships with her siblings, and the impact of her choices on her long-term health: financial, physical, and mental health. Some of our life's journeys will have serious detours which we may never anticipate.

Mine was falling seriously ill.

7. PGROW 2.0

We are almost at the end of the book, and it seemed appropriate to pull the process together, including purpose if you so desire.

i. Reality in Transition

As I decided to leave the corporate world, my reality was that I was a woman with a fairly successful career across multiple international firms, on the wrong side of 50, one who was not a super specialized subject matter expert, yet had a unique way of connecting the dots; who was currently exhausted and not really interested in dealing with the corporate world. I needed to rejuvenate before moving forward. I needed to find my natural optimism and sense of wonder that life had to offer. Repeating -*I needed to find my mojo!*

The usual *tools*, though helpful, don't always provide all the answers:

1. *Self-reflection and mindfulness* were my tools.
2. *Professional help* from my professional colleagues and friends.
3. *Kinesiology, Yoga, and Tai Chi* provided me with *Self-care*.
4. *My tribe* was my bulwark. They are invaluable, and I am eternally grateful to them for being there for me.

One needs to be *ruthless in assessing one's circumstances* – do you need to *get your finances in order*? Sometime back, I was at a women's forum, and I was truly surprised at fairly senior women being somewhat oblivious of the role of financial planning for their professional freedom. When one is younger, there are fewer responsibilities, and the runway is long, so the consequences of a not-so-prudent decision are okay. Work this through. It is an important factor that will stress you.

Do you have *family responsibilities*, and what are your choices in that context? Your goals around these topics are fine, but what is your current reality? Someone I know lives in a place where there are very few families around, which implies that when her young child comes back from school, she needs to be around. She needs to ferry the child to various activities and be available throughout the day. There are creches and nannies, yet it hasn't been enough. The spouse needs to travel a lot. She needs to factor this in as she scripts her way forward.

Irrespective of goals, when choices need to be made, the *gap to goals has to be looked at dispassionately.* I have elder care for my mother now, so when opportunities arise, I need to keep my guardrails of not moving towns or being away from home for more than a couple of days at a time. This implies that my gap to goal has to be thought through from this prism.

Recently, I heard the story of a very successful person in a highly specialized field. He shared his story: after 20+ years of a successful corporate career, he wanted a change. He went back to school and apprenticed at a law firm in London, and 25 years later, he had a very successful second career. He virtually started from scratch. *How many of us have the courage, mindset, and capability to rebuild ourselves to this extent?*

Exercise: *Take a look at your goals from Section 1, and draw up the gap between your current reality and the goal you want to achieve. Is this aligned with your purpose? This is going to be your way to draw up your action plan.*

....

ii. Current Reality Tree [CRT] and Future Reality Tree [FRT]:

CRT and FRT tools are used in the *Theory of Constraints [TOC]* [6] methodology and are used mainly in project management and business. CRT is a tool for diagnosing the root causes of the problems with the object of addressing them. FRT is used for planning and visualizing a future state where these problems are resolved. Their focus is mainly to optimize processes by addressing constraints that impact performance.

I have used this in project management but not for managing my personal goals. Like all things, this framework is helpful in establishing the specific constraints that need to be addressed before moving ahead. It uses the problem statement [in this case, goal], identifies the undesirable effects [UDEs], and establishes a cause-effect structure to address the issues.

By understanding the critical factor causing the problem, it provides a basis for creating solutions.

As I moved through the last couple of years, I realized my biggest hurdle was my mindset, which I had developed from having worked in large organizations for so many years. If I wanted to explore the world, then I truly needed to detoxify the mindset that had grown within me. I needed to look at things with a fresh pair of eyes.

This hit home for me when we were discussing raising money for an educational institution. The bulk of the students who were attending the organization were from families owning small businesses.

The ambitions of the students were to go abroad or work for multinational companies. Yet, if we wanted the parents to pay the institution to build a corpus for entrepreneurship, then they would offer the donations in their family names or organization names. One of the NGOs I worked with accepted these donations and often gave the donors opportunities to put up plaques in their names. For the educational institute, this was seen as being a bit crass and not in line with the more sophisticated institutions that supported Chairs from well-known brands. It made me question – were we being elitist? After all, the parents were genuinely keen to help, so why keep them out?

Taking the same example of the mindset – for me, it was essential to absolutely nurture the growth mindset even though the rest of the world thought it was crazy. This has enabled me to study Quantum sciences from a layperson's perspective and then see how it can be leveraged in business. This has led me to explore contributing to a white paper on the implications of Quantum computing and cybersecurity in the financial sector [yet to be published].

iii. Options for the Way Forward:

Long back, when I was thinking about how to train my team, I was observing them and reflecting on why I kept failing to connect. That's when I had an 'aha' moment:

- **What's my Bus Route?**

Some people take a specific bus/train route to work. They know which route number of buses to take. I remember working with such a person in NY. For years, he had taken the Ferry to Downtown NY and then the subway to mid-town.

Post 9/11, he took the Path to get to work. One day, we hung out together and explored NY, as our office was closed.

As we wandered around NY on foot, I realized I knew the city pretty well as I had explored it every time I spent a weekend there – talking to people and just meandering.

My friend rarely had time to hang out in the city as he had to get back to his family. So, *he knew the bus routes*, not the city!

It was interesting to see how this translated into his work style. He had a certain process of working [aka bus route]. When he worked with people who did not take the 'bus route,' he was not comfortable. This often caused a lot of stress as he was the lead, and the team felt constrained in not being able to have some flexibility.

- **Map to Explore**

Using the example above, I would often go off to the Brooklyn Zoo or the NY Botanical Gardens and then make my way back to downtown Manhattan on foot. The map was my friend; there was structure but immense freedom as well.

It doesn't matter where we are in life; we have an overall construct with people and processes to navigate the world. This is definitely what we learn as leaders. We take stock, do our due diligence, check out, and validate the new environment before moving into action. It doesn't matter which company, which geography, or which function, but there is almost a default way of figuring out the way ahead. This is on auto-pilot every time I join a new board or team.

Figure out the new rules and park them under the standard construct which one uses. I like to look for similarities and differences against my standard and then move ahead.

Every time I have gone through organizational changes, I immediately reset to start this journey. I realize I do something similar in various life situations.

- *Homing pigeon was*

As a kid from an army background who moved to a new city every few years, I had the unconscious skills of a homing pigeon. Wherever I went, I would take stock of where the sun was to orient myself in terms of East / West / North / South. As I walked, I would consciously register landmarks, and I would turn around to ensure I had the view well registered for when I returned. I would even look for 'friendly people' on the way – the street vendor who was kind to kids, the old man walking. I became conscious of this skill when I was in high school in Delhi. I didn't have a map, but I used my instinct to get home. I realize that this skill also translated into other areas of my life. There is an unconscious return to comfort zones, whether it is people, thought processes, locations, etc. Yet, it enables one to explore new territory with more alertness.

- *Type of Path-Finder*

I realized that I was *a homing pigeon with a bias toward map reading*. When I join a new team, I get the lay of the land but then go back to my first principles on what makes sense for me.

This is a good approach when building out options for the future. Sometimes, it's good to use a fixed framework and fill in the blanks on what you want to accomplish.

The map is a stronger approach as you are clear about the destination, and one understands the guardrails to move ahead, but there is flexibility. *The homing pigeon will wing it, and this is great in times of uncertainty.*

What are you? Build your solutions based on your comfort as well as what would work in that situation.

When we first started the off-shoring journey in India, it was a bit of a Homing pigeon approach – lots of experimentation but staying close to customer service, financial acumen, and process discipline to move ahead.

As the industry started growing, there were clear approaches for scaling [maturity models, ISO process standards] to customer-focused solutions [COPC] to clear benchmarks on financials among service providers in the country, across geographies, and industry segments. Today, transition toolboxes are standardized, with strong and detailed approaches for migration of work and then Work Instructions to deliver. So, if one is starting an off-shoring journey today, the first 2 phases are fairly swift before one settles into the delivery phase.

Where are you in your professional journey? What approach would you apply?..........................

8. Swim to the bottom of the pool! Assess the risk

I was in middle school when I started my swimming lessons. I was a good swimmer, yet I would be scared of the depth until I realized that the best way to overcome it was to swim along the bottom of the pool.

Since then, *every time I got into a new pool, I swam along the depths to understand what I was dealing with.* This has become a default even as I developed as a leader *– what was the worst that I needed to deal with?* Having been in financial services virtually all my career, I always check the consequences of going wrong, and that gives me a sense of reverse priority.

I recognize that there are some issues one cannot ignore. In the Indian legal construct, anything to do with Income Tax or Labor laws would be something I would be more alert to as compared to many other issues, as there is often no statute of limitation, and the issues follow you personally and just for the legal entity you operate from.

Again, it's a good way to look at solutions with this lens.

9. Not too hot, not too cold, Just Right – said the Bear!
Pragmatist or Incorrigible Optimist

Whenever we are problem-solving and have to present the solution options, one looks at the '*Risk-Reward' matrix* and creates at least three scenarios. Whenever one is mentoring a start-up to build out the pitch deck, one discusses three options to get a sense of how pragmatic the founder is, whether they understand constraints, and whether they are willing to take the moonshot. It gives us insight into the Founder's mind and whether they understand the business issues clearly.

I am an eternal optimist. I truly believe that things will work out. I use this as a mindset to become more resilient, but I am also a pragmatist at work.

Whether one is working on a personal goal plan or an organizational plan, it is important to see how far we can visualize success. Without pushing forward with this process, one will not be able to see the full possibilities of what one can do. When I started engaging with some people involved with policy work, I wanted to see if I could contribute to ideas that needed to be acted upon now in order to bear fruit 20-25 years from now. I had to believe that decision-makers would be open to the new ideas that I was generating. I needed to push the proposals even if it felt crazy. The first time I did this, I spent a week visualizing all kinds of possibilities; I also got in touch with folks who were good enough to spend time with me as I bounced off the ideas.

I was on a high, and it was super fun – as someone said, 'You seem to be high on some psychedelic drug!' 'Your ideas are like science fiction'. At least one of the ideas got traction, even though it got toned down to a more realistic executable. *Don't be afraid to be the incorrigible optimist* – it may not be appropriate for all situations, yet it enables you to reframe your expectations with the highest potential.

10. Most conservative

This approach is the equivalent of swimming at the bottom of the pool and learning to assess the constraints. Just as one can't always swim at the bottom of the pool and the surface is more fun, we need to use the whole pool!

During the various times when I have gone through mergers and integration, I have got my team to first focus not only on the here-and-now deliverables but also on the future larger opportunities.

That meant survival. It also demonstrates that one is firmly grounded in reality and that there is no waste of resources and survival is prioritized, yet one is looking for growth.

As I have a portfolio of business commitments, it is important to *understand this 'floor' for each activity*. For example, I need to attend all board meetings with enough preparation. So, unless it's a very serious emergency, I will not miss these meetings.

For mentoring, I will say 'x' number of hours, especially where I am an anchor mentor for the founders – i.e., there is a long-term commitment. Other initiatives will scale up and down depending on demand. Of course, this is easy to draw up when one is building a financial model for a business. Do you want more or less leverage? What is the commitment that you have made to the investors with respect to profitability or break-even? It is more complex as we add other variables like ESG, CSR, DEI, etc.

11. Realistic - 'The porridge is just right – not too hot or cold'

Writing this book was an unrealistic time commitment. I assumed that I could continue with all my activities plus just throw in a couple of hours for the book! I told myself that I could commit to writing 3-4 hours a day, 3 or 4 days a week, and get the book done.

What I did not anticipate was that my eyes would get really fatigued staring at the screen so intensely at night. It is vastly different from doing emails, decks, or video calls. I did not incorporate the time needed for research or bouncing ideas off people. *Finally, I felt this crushing level of stress to finish it.* I often had no clue as to how to find good examples. I did not have the skills/craft for writing. Like all competencies, this needs to be developed. Hence, *my Time Planning around this effort was completely out of sync with reality!*

This is often the case when companies are scaling up. The initial focus is on getting customers, yet once this starts gaining momentum, the ability to fulfill the orders becomes a challenge. The team struggles to deliver. The processes, systems, and trained personnel are just getting synergized, so often, there are breaks. If a process usually takes 10-15% of the total effort during the initial scale-up, it can take up to 30% or even more as skills, processes, and systems are still being developed.

So, as you work out your options, consider this inflation into your time/effort and even your financials in your possible solutions. This is vital for success.

12. Creating the Paths

Your *Goal* is established, yet are you really clear about the *outcomes*? We often say that we want interesting work. We want meaningful work. We want to make a difference – can you articulate what that will look like? Can you define it with an example? How will you know you have achieved it?

As someone described it – a goal is something you want to accomplish, whereas an outcome is what happens when a goal is achieved. *My goal is to hatch a number of butterflies.*

The outcome is to have a butterfly garden.

i. Understanding the Problem or Opportunity

That's is the first step. In our context, do we understand what our barriers to achieving the goal are? Do you understand the steps to be taken to get to the goal?

One of the things that I was told was to get onto Boards. Go to a head-hunter; maybe that will help. Else, see if anyone in your circle is aware of you wanting to join a Board.

Do you have the credentials? One of my friends saw my LinkedIn profile and said, "Hey, your profile does not look like you are an Independent Director.

Write that up appropriately. Register with the national Independent Director database."

Make sure you are eligible. I have been on boards since 1982, yet

I was told that it might be better to do the exam to demonstrate competence – I bit the bullet and executed.

ii. Information is King or Queen or...!

In today's digital age, it's important to understand the context surrounding a situation, statement, or context, and this can be done through relevant data from reliable sources and fact-checking.

Research and consult experts and seek input from reliable sources. Then, **Brainstorm options, evaluate the pros and cons, prioritize values and criteria, narrow down options, review, and generate more options. Kick the tires and seek input. Consider the trade-off.**

My goal as I transitioned was, *"I want a second career that makes me create abundance and be involved in areas of long-term impact."* To achieve this, I could:

- Find another job
- Start a business
- Start an NGO / Impact activity / Fund
- Create a portfolio of activities where:
- I will charge the market price/value-added price
- For other services, I will provide them at a cost
- For the social sector, I will offer my services for free

This was based on advice from many people, and this has helped me feel more balanced about how I go about delivering what I do.

If I want to say NO, I check if it is creating Abundance. Sometimes, doing a large amount of evaluation of start-ups to get them through a pipeline supports creating abundance through a selection of the cohort.

Yet, if it truly drains my energy on a daily basis, then it is not the right action for me.

Exercise:

1. *Write down what you want your legacy to be.* ....
2. *Do you have a purpose in life? yes / no* ......
   a. *If yes, what is it?* ....

b. If no, do you think you need a purpose ....

This is a good understanding of what your Purpose could be - don't overthink.

Conclusion:

Life is a journey, and it is important to see if *you want to drive it or just go with the flow.* I think both are fine. If you are reading this book, you want to consciously push ahead, explore, and try some of these techniques and see where you land. Go back to the first exercise of PGROW for the last chapter.

8
BEING A WOMAN PROFESSIONAL

Right from a young age, I have felt very acutely that, as human beings, we all need to have our freedom and the right to equal opportunity. Being an army brat, my primary sense of identity was that of an Indian; other identities were not as important. Being an only child, there were no gender expectations except to occasionally wear traditional dresses.

My ideal at one time was James Barry, a military surgeon who hid her female identity. She was discovered as a female only after a post-mortem. For a young girl where the external world puts a lot of restrictions, this seemed the most adventurous and practical way to achieve what one wanted! Today, I feel bad that she could not live freely enough to be the doctor that she wanted to be.

Today, Vagambrini, a female Rishi from the Rig Veda who wrote Devi Suktam, appeals to me. Her words are still alive today – read daily and sung during festivals. The deep insight and poetry make one marvel. What a powerful impact by someone from the 'dawn of civilization.' I doubt whether my words will stay through the next digital cycle

There is a lot of effort going on to support gender equality, equity, and inclusion for all.

Each of our stories is different and yet the same. Some of our gender roles are evolutionary driven by biology – childbearing. The cultures to which we belong have their own mores. With technology, some of the natural restrictions no longer pose an issue. Despite all the strides, in practice, it is varied, and studies show that we still have 250+ years to catch up financially at the workplace. Add to that, one's family dynamics shape us.

Each family is different. Formal workplaces legally support equality, yet there are cultural, conscious, and unconscious biases. We may want to call out injustice, yet most of the time, we are all victims of our own social constructs.

Aspects of the gender lens to consider when making career choices and goals.

What are the dynamics at play from a gender perspective in your current situation, not what is ideal but your current reality?

As a senior leader, I always wanted to make sure we had a level field. I remember once being introduced as a 'female MD' yet again. I was tired and had enough of this, so I said, "Would you call me a gay MD or a blind MD if I was visually impaired or part of the LGBTQ+ community?"

Another time at a dinner, someone introduced the only other woman there to me as a "diversity person." I was infuriated – as an MD, I could call it out, whereas the lone young woman had just accepted it. We still have a long way to go.

Finally, when it came to my decisions around elder care, I made sure that I stayed in the professional world but took on a role that enabled me to put my family first, not because of any social pressures but simply because I could not have lived with myself if I did not take on that responsibility in the manner that I did. It was based on who I am and what would work for me.

Workplace dynamics have changed. Quite often, when it comes to caregiving, women tend to play a disproportionate role. Yet, in my career, I have repeatedly seen men taking on the role of caregivers often while pivoting their careers to manage the situation.

There is an evolving fluidity, and stereotypes may not always represent the current reality.

Despite this, one area where there is still a lot of reticence is the female biological process and its impact on one's professional career. The younger generation is more open about some of these discussions. As an employer, one wants to be inclusive, yet this topic throws up issues that society is still trying to engage with in a pragmatic manner. Is this a factor that you need to consider in the context of your career? We hear a lot about the implications of PCOS among young women. Is that a factor? In parallel, there is more research on female health; *[my favorite female health-related video is by Dr Sara Gottfried [1]].*

Gender roles – many women become the primary career owners in the family unit. Not many men are openly calling out to say that they want to be stay-at-home partners, even if they opt for a less stressful role.

Exercise:

Write down your Purpose or Goal around Gender related aspects. Identify what beliefs and how does it help you or hinder you in your growth. Write down WHY this is important. Then, leverage your PGROW technique to identify the gap between your current reality and goal. Then, check how this may affect your professional goals. Do you have a specific gender-linked

1. *Goals...*
2. *Beliefs...*
3. *Why you need to do something......................................*
4. *How will this impact your career choices.........................*

1. Women and Other Inclusive Networks

I have stayed involved with a number of **Women's networks** as I believe in supporting the DEI. My engagement tends to be through speaking to different groups or being part of forums that drive these interests. The other day, someone said," Why are you on X board? It's not such an important company". I realized I enjoyed the fact that the founder was a strong, ambitious woman who drove growth.

I wanted to support her success. *One doesn't need to be aggressive about driving the women's agenda – just get involved to the extent you can.* You will find yourself richly rewarded by so many people.

The other day, I wanted some guidance on how I could raise money for a longitudinal study on women's savings habits based on the central bank's report. Just pinging a few people got me rapid suggestions and offers of help. In my experience, more people are willing to help than we expect. Of course, **the unwritten rule is, do you also contribute to the network?** This is true for any community you may want to support, be it LGBTQ+, people with disability, etc.

2. Am I a Feminist?

I don't know, as the definitions have evolved over the years.

I believe all human beings need to be liberated. *Everyone is a product of their upbringing, culture, evolution, and expectations. It is for us to choose how we want to grow – as a victim or as a warrior.*

There are serious structural inequities for women and other DEI groups, and the challenges differ widely across cultures, economic strata, educational backgrounds, etc. Many of these structural differences are getting addressed in law and in the dictums of society, but the unconscious blockers are yet to be tackled. Again, a lot of enablers, such as affirmative action, are being put in place, and society is still internalizing its response. With technology, many of the barriers to gender-linked work have disappeared, but the mindset is yet to catch up.

As a young individual, I devoured all the feminist literature – often feeling overwhelmed by the inequities in society.

I chose to focus on building my independence, whether through a career leading to financial independence or cultivating a mindset of owning my decisions and actions. I was fortunate to have great role models among my family members and the community I grew up in.

In my career, I had active organizational support to recruit women, even in organizations where it was not common. Thus, I was able to build my professional tribe in each company where I worked. As I grew more senior in my roles, I had both the opportunity and responsibility to take a DEI leadership role actively both within the organization and the ecosystem.

The first chance I had to step up as a champion for women was when a young woman from one of the multinationals was killed going home. I contacted the Chairman and offered to speak to the women in the company, and along with Latika Pai, I agreed to address the press.

The story did not garner as much attention as there was another incident that day about female cops in a small town chasing romancing couples in a park! Thus began my tryst with various women's initiatives. *If you can speak up or provide support for others, do so. Stand-up.*

Over the years, I took on roles in industry bodies such as NASSCOM and CII, from leading the DEI Steering Committees to being a jury member to identify best practices or being a speaker in many forums. I was part of AnitaB.org, a forum for women in technology, apart from other women's forums.

I was active with Avtar – a women's recruitment agency that has morphed into an amazing space for thought leadership in DEI.

I was involved as a speaker with a number of the IIM Bangalore women's programs. Whether it was Thomson Reuters or Deutsche, I was active in pushing this agenda. During this phase, my brand of feminism has been Western Liberal feminism with an Indian flavor.

In 2014, when Ravneet Gill got me onto the bank board in India, the task at hand was to increase the number of women on that board. Within a year, we had ~40% women on the India board, which was well recognized in The Economic Times, India. I became a 'masthead' for that issue.

As we headed toward Covid, my engagement turned towards mentoring, and this has been my mainstay even as I have transitioned out of the corporate world.

2023 Women's Day was almost a watershed for me as it hit me that I am involved in truly diverse efforts. I started the day with an event with a government's Self-Help Group. I then joined a celebration at a small Business school where the unseen women were recognized—cleaners, gardeners, cooks, and not just students and academics. In the afternoon, I moderated a panel of women lawyers and scientists on behalf of the Indian Intellectual Property Office. IP lawyers spoke about the World Intellectual Property Office's programs to increase women's participation globally, while the women scientists were concerned that this type of affirmative action could potentially dilute the quality. I wrapped up the day as part of a panel discussion with a multinational company. Despite all the progress, the *shift is still needed both personally and organizationally.*

3. The Reality of Transitioning from the Corporate World

As I left my corporate career, I was getting asked to lead women's programs. Like all the other dimensions of one's life, think about what is important to you on this front. When getting asked to lead 'Women's programs,' it was as though I had some great insight into over 50% of humankind just because I am female. Be real! Further, it was as though my entire professional career in financial services, technology, operations, risk, and strategy was irrelevant. My only identity was that of a female!

I am actively involved in supporting women through mentoring, investing, and supporting the ecosystem changes. Yet my Professional Identity is that of a Senior Leader coming from the financial sector - not a female. I was clear that my primary roles would be like the TiE Bangalore Board member and FinTech Chair, etc. – I.e., gender agnostic.

Organizations offer protection – can networks do the same? As I left the corporate world, it hit me that I did not have the corporate air cover to handle the day-to-day issues. There are no guidelines and no points of escalation. You have to use your common sense. I have been talking to 100s of founders and happily sharing my phone number. Yet, with one person, I did not do so. I even met him with another investor in a public place, but all interactions were via mail. One day, he wanted an urgent meeting, and when we got on the Zoom call, he started getting abusive and angry as he was not getting funding or support to move forward.

Listen to your instincts – evolution has given you the tools.

Most of my mentoring efforts happen through organizations, IIMB NSRCEL, TiE, Angel Networks, and direct referrals from known people.

Until this point, I had been on boards predominantly as a whole-time executive director and a few as an independent board member. Now, I am being sought after as a woman independent director. Today, when I join a board, I actively work to establish my professional contribution before pushing the women's agenda. I prefer to wait and see if they are ready for the inclusion discussions.

In my post-corporate phase, I am discovering new approaches to the gender equity agenda. One such exploration is to support gender-linked Behavioural Economic studies. ASIA, the think tank I am part of, has embarked on a study to understand the behavior of educated, young, urban women and their savings, investments, and spending patterns. While there is a plethora of gender studies, there are very few papers on gender behavioral economics. Policymakers and banks create a lot of products and solutions for women, but they are not based on gender-linked behavioral economic studies.

Today, it is no longer about women getting into the workforce, but ensuring that women's requirements are considered in all fields, including medical research or in female 'crash' dummies to test vehicular safety. *Times are Changing!*

4. Sensitive issues

More and more women are joining the workforce. Glass ceilings are being broken, as per McKinsey's Women in the Workplace 2023 report. The issues are more about the 'broken rung' and microaggression, which deplete one's energy.

Additionally, during Covid, awareness on mental health increased. Being a Mental Health First Aid Provider – one learns that in many mental health disorders, the percentage of women who are affected tends to be higher than that of men.

Given all of this, for an employer, especially small companies and those adhering to the SDG goals [*Sustainable Development Goals*], the pressure to be compliant is tough.

I was talking to a female MD who leads a growing organization, and her reaction was very telling. She said, "S, I actively recruit women. Yet on a practical level, I am stressed with all the new expectations. It is almost as though the environment is using this new inclusive approach to keep women out."

5. The conflict between personal stand vs. organizational requirements and the role of NGOs

Being part of SVP, I see a group of volunteers who work with NGOs in the Social Justice sphere. I am incredibly impressed with the work they do. Every time they are able to rescue young women from human trafficking, one feels happy, but this is not even a small drop in the ocean. These are the people one turns to when dealing with difficult situations.

One of the joys of a long career is dealing with complex issues. There was a situation that might have been a case of 'honor killing.' As an organization, we could not take any action as there was no data to support this common belief. Yet I could not leave it, so we tried to contact some NGOs involved in this area to take this up.

In another situation, there was a young woman from a very difficult family background who could not cope with the work pressure. At home, she was told that if she lost her job, she would need to move out of the house. She was under tremendous pressure. At this point, she saw that a colleague had left some money lying around. In a moment of impulse, she decided to take the money to use as a deposit for getting a paying guest accommodation. When caught, she offered to pay it back, but it was a legal case of theft. We also knew that if this young woman got into the prison system, her life would have been ruined. We tried to work through an NGO to resolve this.

Pervasive Sexism is a term that I came across when looking at some gender studies. When I look back over the years, this has existed in many flavors - from simple mansplaining to outright in-your-face sexual harassment. For me, the microaggression and the way it would get deflected was most tiring. I have been on both the receiving end and have had to call out this behavior in the organization. Today, I even talk to my mother's doctor to take a stand.

6. Disability, LGBT+ and Aging

While I have focused on the gender lens, other forms of DEI are also close to me. As I was building teams, I recognized that people with disabilities were equally competent and amazingly committed. We tried to encourage inclusion through various programs. I will always be proud of the HR team at Thomson Reuters, who won the Hellen Keller award in the midst of the integration. Obviously, the number of staff with disability was not many. At Deutsche Bank, too, we won many awards for supporting people with disabilities. Today, I am a Friend of AssisTech Foundation [ATF], and I mentor start-ups in this field.

My attitude toward transgender was shaped by my father, who explained the concept of gender dysphoria when I was in my teens. At work, when we formed the global DEI councils, I was always conscious that there were many countries where the LGBTQ+ conversation could put them at risk with the law. Being allies to the LGBTG+ community was a natural evolution. *Being human is a superset to all identities.*

Recently, as part of Social Venture Partners, we were funding an NGO that was developing entrepreneurial skills among sex workers. When asked about other funders, we were told that today, companies are willing to support LGBTQ+ programs and women's programs. *The issue of social justice is truly complex and often very disturbing. Hats off to all those who work in this field.*

Last year, I was on a flight, and a man who had worked for me sat next to me and asked – "I am told that we cannot hire anyone over 35 in the following fields, and I will attain that age soon. What do I do?"

I heard a FinTech founder rant at the central bank regulator as he felt 60-year-olds could not understand what makes start-ups successful. For once, the reporter seemed stunned! *Age used to be associated with knowledge and wisdom, yet today, it is linked to redundancy, especially in the professional world. Time for recasting?*

7. Why and What of DEI

This is a book on change. As per the World Economic Forum's Global Gender Gap 2021 report, it will take almost 257 years for men and women to have equal pay. If we add the lens of disability, LGBTQ+, ageism, and other aspects into this challenge, the human race has a long way to go.

i. One is not enough!

Token women in positions of authority is not good enough. Every decision-making body needs functional representation with adequate women [other groups] in the roles. I found that if there was a critical mass of women in functional roles, gender would become irrelevant.

Have a critical mass of gender representation in decision-making bodies and roles.

ii. Education and Financial Independence

Make sure you and the people around you have both. I am not just talking about learning whatever is written in the book but being educated about your rights and what is owed to you in every formal construct – employment contract, marriage, insurance, etc.

iii. Speak-Up, Act, Refer issues to organizations dealing with change

If you are in a difficult spot, speak up and reach out to people for help. Even if you don't want to complain, tell people in authority so that when the time comes, they can act. Change has to happen. *Don't waste time on the 'victim mindset' – focus on the outcome you want. You can cry or find the humor when it is all over.*

iv. Help where you can, and if you need to balance your organization, family, and other needs, do so.

A young woman came to me in panic. She was being pressured by her family to marry an unsavory character.

The first time she came, I heard her out. The next time, she said that this man's friends had followed her to work, and they were lurking outside. She did not want to go to the cops. We gave her the contact information of an NGO that worked on social justice matters. She said she would go to them. Due to confidentiality issues, we could not follow up further. *Help if you can*

    v. Are women vulnerable targets? Maybe, but that does not make them weak. Operate from strength.

In one of the places I worked, we were at the cusp of scale-up, and we had recruited a very smart and capable woman leader. She came in and put in a lot of systems necessary for growth.

The folks who were used to working in a more relaxed way did not like it. We then had our annual employee survey, and an overwhelming majority targeted her. Interestingly, her male colleagues all spoke up for her and pointed out that she was being unfairly targeted. We called the team and told them that if they had genuine issues, then they could talk, in confidence, with one of the tenured trusted managers. No one came forward. The lady manager was devasted by this personal attack and wanted to leave. I spoke to her to face the crowd and stay for a year before leaving. She stayed for a year and then left. She continues to be a very successful leader. I don't know if a male leader would have been targeted so viciously. We need to stand up for those unfairly targeted.

    vi. Networks are great support!

At Thomson Financial, a significant number of the global executive committee under Sharon Rowlands were women. We rarely spoke of women's empowerment as it was very visible. As the Thomson Reuters merger progressed, the ratio of CXO-level women dropped to resemble the corporate world of 2008. Though we had a substantial female workforce at the lower levels, we had very few female leaders. However, our programs for mentoring and developing women have increased. That is when I met Prof (Dr) Vasanthi Srinivasan and heard her speak about the primary identities of women vs men, which I wrote about earlier.

At one time in my career, I had a number of stalking calls, and I had to go to the cops to get it addressed. It is definitely disturbing when someone calls and says they know where you live and who all are at home. Be pragmatic and build your network to include people who can help. I also channeled my grandmother, who was a tough lady ready to confront.

 vii. *Use your common sense, listen to your gut.*
 viii. **Cyberstalking** -*Block and report. Do not engage.*

Conclusion

Gender dialogue is active in public life – whether it is about effective global women leaders tackling Covid, the US Senate hearings on Gender Theory, Identity, and associated topics, or the Kenyan senator Gloria Orwoba [2] in February 2023 speaking up against 'period shame.'

This book is about change and transition, and gender awareness is a vital foundation for owning your destiny and not living like a victim. Yes, there are many more complex and uncomfortable challenges to address, but learn to be like a warrior and not like a victim; for that, just be self-aware.

9
CALL TO ACTION: WAY FORWARD

You probably picked up the book because you were at a cusp of change, or maybe your career felt "GREY" like mine did, or you did not feel you were learning enough, making enough impact, enjoying your professional journey, or maybe you were mad at the people around you.

Have you started making changes? If not, do it now! Don't waste time being stuck – it takes only *a little effort to live intentionally*.

The world is not going to wait for you to get ready – it is in a constant whirl, and if you want to be part of that dance, you need to move. The old book, *"Who Moved My Cheese?"* by Dr Spencer Johnson [1], speaks about the importance of responding to change proactively.

With rapid changes across every spectrum of our professional life, including the AI disruption – if you don't set your pace, your own goals, and your definition of success, then it will be tough. *Own yourself!*

Use the following, *or not*, but find the way to define the best version of yourself. *It is your life!*

A Self-Defined Future – try at least some of these questions and see where you go!

1. What are the three things that you started/stopped/changed as you read the book? It could also be what you liked or hated. *It is all about – did it move you?*
   * a. ....
   * b. ....
   * c. ....

2. If you have not yet started, then do something to *shift your energy* to *your current state of being*. What will it be?
   * a. Today..
   * b. This week..
   * c. This month......................................

3. **Purpose** – Do you have clarity about this? If yes, you are truly amazing and blessed. Give yourself a high five! If not, don't sweat it. It will come.

4. What is the *issue that is bothering you*? Keeping you stuck? Making you feel down? Pick the issues that come to mind now, and you can always use tools to help if you want.
   * a. ....
   * b. ....
   * c. ....
   * d. ....

5. *Can you re-frame your issues into outcome statements?* The brain does not understand negative statements or future/ past – frame it in the present. You are setting your intention, goal, and aspiration.
   * a. From now, I will ....

6. *What are your blockers?* (Both practical and emotional). What are you going to do to address it? Leave it or act? This could be an item for **PGROW**.
   Blockers / Emotions Actions to address
       a. ....
       b. ....
       c. ....

7. *Are you still feeling 'Blah!'?* Do you want to do something about it? If you are already doing something – then celebrate! This is important. If no, then
   a. Have you identified the issue..........................
   b. Do you need professional help........................
   c. Do you have a trusted partner with whom you can discuss this and take it forward? *This need not be your close family, yet often they can surprise you with their unstinting support. Or it might be your trusted friend or even you*
   ....
   d. Do you have your personal board of directors? If not, you can start building now! ....
   e. Do you have energy vampires that bring you down further? – they are not the folks to go to at this time.
   f. What action will you take to move ahead? What action can you take?..
   g. Do you have a pacer? Can any App help you? ....

8. *Next steps to shift you from low to top gear.* Write it down:
   a. What is the help you need? *Without this clarity, you could go to the wrong person or get the incorrect support.*
   b. What action can you take...........................
   c. What action will you take...........................
   d. Do you just want it to fester........................
   e. Does it just need to wait ....

Ownership of your strengths and weaknesses

9. *Do you know your strengths?* If not, use Strength Finder [2] or any other tool to understand your strengths. Your boss, colleagues, and trusted friends can all provide insights.
    a.   List down your strengths:
    i. …………..
    ii. …………..
    iii. ………….. ..
    b.   What are you doing to nurture and improve your strengths so that they can be exponential? Huh? *Yes, this is important. It is not enough to have the strengths; like a muscle, it needs to be regularly exercised and fed the right food for it to be at its best. Can you strengthen*
    i.   Nurturing activities
    ii. Strengthen activities
    iii. …………………….....

10. *Have you identified your weakness?* If not, do you want to? You can use the same tools to identify your strengths. Now List them:
    i. …………..
    ii. …………..
    iii. …………..
    a.   Can the weaknesses seriously trip you up as a professional? If yes, can you fix it so that it will not be a hindrance? *It does not need to be your strength. Tiger Woods is never going to be a top cricketer, but he could play.*
    b.   List the weakness you want to address:
    Weakness | Potential action & how will you measure progress
    i.   ………......
    ii. …………..
    iii. …………..
    If not, then park it for another day.
    I am never going to ace Calculus! I can live with it.

11. Do you know the kind of role you want to play in your goal?
    a. Layperson, subject matter expert, project manager - what do you want to bring to the table? ....

12. Have you aligned *your professional goal with your other goals and values?* Let us keep it simple
    a. Are your goals aligned – Yes/ No
    b. Any action required?
        i. Financial ....
        ii. Mental, emotional, physical, spiritual.............. .
        iii. Relationship goals....................................
        iv. Other goals.. ..
        v. Values ....

13. Do you know *how you handle different experiences*? If not, write it down and validate it with your trusted advisors
    a. Do you react or respond? ....
    b. Do you jump into action? ....
    c. When you jump into action, is it just an impulsive decision?..................
    d. Do you really want to explore possibilities? ....
    e. Do you regularly procrastinate on everything or just some things? ....
    f. Do you constantly keep on analyzing before acting? ....
    g. Do you feel emotionally paralyzed? ....
    h. Do you want to use some of the tools from the book to build your self-awareness? *Only with awareness can you be in charge of yourself.*

14. *Networks* -list down your support and challenge networks
    a. Support network ....
    b. Challenge network......

15. *Acceptance of Change and Resilience* – be the martial artist: set your goal and then practice, practice, practice. Get your checklist and

tick off all the things you did. Did you at least make your bed today? Tell me yes!

16. If you could miraculously *leave your baggage behind* – *what would it be?* Write down only what is weighing you down. This is not a laundry list.
    a. ....
    b. ....
    c. ....

17. *New door?* Do you want to try new things? If not – it's perfectly fine as long as you are happy, but you picked up this book – so maybe you want to explore. If yes, list the possible 'new doors' you want to open.
    a. ....
    b. ....
    c. ....

18. Re-enforce your growth mindset – *even if you did nothing else from this checklist.*
    Please build a growth mindset. You can do this by jotting down some things that you learned and which you have put into action. It is a good way to reinforce that *you are investing in yourself to shift and change.* It is important to acknowledge even small shifts. You may have started to do an activity and then realized, "Oh my god, I haven't thought about this perspective before," and that's the magic of it because you may get a lot of new ideas as you start your self-exploration journey.
    a. *Write down two or three takeaways that you received in your self-exploration journey in the last month or so*...............
    b. *Start a Growth mindset journal, blog, or podcast*..........

19. Success criteria - *Define the success you want to achieve – on your terms, not how someone else defines it for you.* It can just be the activity for the day, or it may be a major deliverable.

Keep the energy moving forward.
  a. What will make you feel successful today?
  ....

20. Permission to rest, sleep, and do nothing — have you scheduled this yet?
  ....

21. Prune your to-do list; start with what is essential; the rest will get addressed with time.

22. **PGROW is a simple tool.** If you have not already started using it – try it.
  a. *What is your professional goal?* ....
  b. *What is your current reality?* ....
  c. *What is your gap to goal?* ....
  d. *What are your options to bridge this gap to goal?*
  ....
  e. *From your list of options to move forward:*
    i. *Identify the set of items that you don't want to deal with or*........ ....
    ii. *Want to procrastinate, and*..
    iii. *List the reasons for your reluctance to act*..
  f. **WAY FORWARD: Build the Elephant one bite at a time – from the Option you have selected**
    i. Break it into small activities, and start acting on the next few steps.
    ii. ACT on it every day
    iii. Monitor progress
    iv. Course correct / drop it if that is what is right

23. *Celebration*
  a. How do you celebrate? Consciously using this will help you.

Please list the way ……...............................
It could be anything like hugging your dog, eating ice cream, doing a dance, talking to your loved one, basking in their support, etc.

    b.   Who is with you in this celebration? If you don't have anyone, don't worry – the world is out there with you……

This chapter is not meant to be a workbook; you can use it as such, but as a way for you to shift.

These types of tools have helped me. I hope they will help you as well.

Joys of Dreaming and Visualizing

This book would not be complete without talking about dreaming and visualizing.

Don Miguel Ruiz's *"The Four Agreements"* [3], based on the Toltec philosophy of dreaming, is "similar to starring in our own movie following a script we write ourselves." To some extent, that is what we are attempting to do – for that, the joy of dreaming is a must.

The first thing I do when I start mentoring a start-up is to ask them to share their dream, their vision, and maybe even their purpose.

That point is where all possibilities exist – the egg before the pupae and butterfly. This is a point of just joy. As children, we had it. As adults, we have forgotten that.

Find that space. Wishing is not enough; link that dream to visualization in practical terms.

Test your dream against reality as you visualize it, and keep refining it until you have a plan. ***Identify your eggs to hatch your butterflies!***

Do you pivot?

I have no idea what you should do - it's your journey and your life!

I have to start my next sprint! I thought I had a great portfolio of professional activities: independent directorships, startup activities, and my engagement with the think-tank. As my mother ages, she needs my support more.

I did not bargain for being part of the fun ride to organizing the TiE Global Summit 2024, coming up with 6000 delegates over a week by the end of the year; there are discussions of setting up a new institution. I need to re-balance my life again! I need to reassess what will make me happy and fulfilled. This is the start of the next adventure.

As we attempt to live life with intentionality, things happen, and we need to adjust, stay resilient, and grow. To get through this roller-coaster ride, here is my version of the serenity prayer:

May I have the Serenity to accept the things I cannot Change
The Courage to Change the things I can and
Wisdom to know the difference.

Thank you so much for buying and reading this book. I wish you all the very best for your transformational journey!

Appendix

Chapter 1: The Transition: Goals & Current Reality
[1] https://bitly.ws/3dD5M
[2] https://bitly.ws/3dD5V
[3] https://bitly.ws/3dIBv
[4] https://bitly.ws/3dD6c
[5] https://bitly.ws/3dD6f
[6] https://bitly.ws/3dD6k
[7] https://bitly.ws/3dD6r
[8] https://bitly.ws/3dD6y
[9] https://bitly.ws/3dD6E
[10] https://bitly.ws/3d4W2
[11] https://bitly.ws/3dIBd
[12] https://bitly.ws/3dD6V
[13] https://bitly.ws/3dD7a
[14] https://bitly.ws/3dD7g

Chapter 2: You are more than your Career
[1] https://bitly.ws/3d4ZE
[2] https://bitly.ws/3dD97
[3] https://bitly.ws/3dD9a
[4] https://bitly.ws/3dD9e
[5] https://bitly.ws/3dD9k
[6] https://bitly.ws/3d53a
[7] https://bitly.ws/3dDa3
[8] https://bitly.ws/3d547
[9] https://bitly.ws/3d54h
[10] https://bitly.ws/3dIz7
[11] https://bitly.ws/3dD8s
[12] https://bitly.ws/3dD8z
[13] https://bitly.ws/3dD8E
[14] https://bitly.ws/3dD8V
[15] https://bitly.ws/3dD9q

[16] https://bitly.ws/3dD9U
[17] https://bitly.ws/3d53r
[18] https://bitly.ws/3dD9I

Chapter 3: Values and Beliefs: The "Why" of Goals
[1] https://bitly.ws/3dDaX
[2] https://bitly.ws/3dDaY

Chapter 4: Choice to Decision-making
[1] https://bitly.ws/3dDbw
[2] https://bitly.ws/3dDbI
[3] https://bitly.ws/3dDbF
[4] https://bitly.ws/3dDbN
[5] https://bitly.ws/3dDbW
[6] https://bitly.ws/3dDbr
[7] https://bitly.ws/3dDc7

Chapter 5: Networking: The Hidden Influences
[1] https://bitly.ws/3dDdA
[2] https://bitly.ws/3dDdE
[3] https://bitly.ws/3dIIs
[4] https://bitly.ws/3dDdI
[5] https://bitly.ws/3dDdM

Chapter 6: Thriving in Uncertainty

[1] https://bitly.ws/3dDe5
[2] https://bitly.ws/3dIJQ
[3] https://bitly.ws/3dDee
[4] https://bitly.ws/3dDem
[5] https://bitly.ws/3dDet
[6] https://bitly.ws/3dDeB
[7] https://bitly.ws/3dDeK
[8] https://bitly.ws/3dDeS

Chapter 7 Purpose: Your Bedrock to Change

[1] https://bitly.ws/3dDfp
[2] https://bitly.ws/3dIKa
[3] https://bitly.ws/3dDfR
[4] https://bitly.ws/3dDg2
[5] https://bitly.ws/3dDgc
[6] https://bitly.ws/3dDgn

Chapter 8: Being a Female Professional

[1] https://bitly.ws/3dDh8
[2] https://bitly.ws/3dDgQ

Chapter 9: Call to Action: Way Forward

[1] https://bitly.ws/3dDhi
[2] https://bitly.ws/3dDhn
[3] https://bitly.ws/3dDhz

ABOUT THE AUTHOR

Sandhya, after 37 years of Corporate life, as a Global, APAC and India leader with Deutsche Bank, Thomson Reuters, AXA / Guardian Royal Exchange and TVS group decided to explore new avenues.

Sandhya's corporate career covered financial services; off-shoring / shared services; operations and technology; risk, regulatory governance; strategy, innovation and digitalization and social impact initiatives. She has been an MD since 2001, and in 2021 she felt the urge to explore new paths that would give her the opportunity to learn and create abundance where possible. Sandhya's passion has been innovation, growth and change / transformation with a strong bent towards impact and inclusion. With these guiding principles, Sandhya has built a professional portfolio ranging from being an Independent Director on listed, public, private companies to being on the Board of non-profits / educational institution. She actively supports the start-up ecosystem and mentors startups, scale-ups and social ventures through strategic consulting. She is on the board of a national think-tank as a Distinguished Professor apart from championing various causes: Diversity, Equity and Inclusion, Intellectual Property and growth of Quantum in the country to name a few.

Sandhya's experience as a senior leader coupled with her wide-ranging interests enables her to link networks, ecosystems and provides unique perspectives to promote growth and change. Her ability to focus on execution in the present while evolving a vision for the future makes her distinctive.

Life is a journey and the adventure continues!

www.ingramcontent.com/pod-product-compliance
Lightning Source LLC
LaVergne TN
LVHW041333080426
835512LV00006B/427